Daniil Khanin

UNIT ECONOMICS

Data Driven Decisions
for Business and Startups

Unit economics. Data Driven Decisions for Business and Startups
by Daniil Khanin

Translate: Tatyana Zharova
Illustrators: Daniil Khain

ISBN[en]:979-8-8793-1775-6
ISBN[ru]:978-5-0060-2245-4

To my girls,
Varvara and Alexandra

Table of contents

Foreword by Ash Maurya

Running a business without metrics is like flying a plane without instruments. Neither is a good idea when visibility is low. This is especially true in startups and early-stage products that operate in a constant fog of uncertainty as they frantically search for a repeatable and scalable business model.

But while measuring metrics used to be difficult, the pendulum has swung the other way. Today, it's possible to measure every click on a website and user action. This explosion in metrics data, however, hasn't resulted in more clarity. We now drown in a sea of non-actionable data.

Enter Unit Economics. In this book, Daniil shows you how to cut through this facade of vanity metrics and instead measure the output of a working business model using a handful of metrics that measure a product's unit economics.

He shows you how to baseline growth and extrapolate performance from these unit economics. Along the way, he demystifies often misunderstood concepts like customer acquisition cost, lifetime value, and contribution margin with simple visuals that help you both internalize these metrics and learn how to measure them correctly.

He shares my love for Goldratt's theory of constraints as it applies to optimizing business models. Too many entrepreneurs (and advisors) simply guess at what's riskiest in a business model. But the stakes are too high for guessing incorrectly. When a startup prioritizes the wrong risks, it wastes already limited resources on suboptimal efforts that shorten its runway.

Daniil shows you a better approach that doesn't rely on guessing. He shows you how to lay out a product's unit metrics, like a series of steps on a factory floor, and systematically identify the slowest step or weakest link. Working on anything else, but the weakest link is premature optimization.

He highlights the importance of measuring your metrics as batches or cohorts and shows you how to normalize and attribute causality between user actions and business model results.

He ends the book by showing you how to turn your unit economics model into a full-blown financial model that you can share with investors to communicate your product's value and growth potential.

Unit Economics is a practical handbook for anyone who wants to make better data-driven product and growth decisions. I hope you'll implement his practical guidance and help pave the way to a world with better products for all.

Not more numbers, but actionable metrics.

Ash Maurya
March 16, 2024
Austin, TX

Preface to the English edition

This book was born out of nearly a decade of formalizing a methodology for optimizing product development through a system of easy-to-understand metrics that can be managed by any team launching business projects.

Over the years, I have developed a large number of techniques and approaches that allow using simple and understandable metrics available to any team at the very start to create an idea of what kind of business they can build, assess the market, create a financial model, and start managing their tasks.

At the same time, it is necessary to mention the fact that this methodology is a development of the original approach proposed by David Skok, formulated in the product approach by Ilya Krasinski and brought to a ready-made set of tools by me. Ilya and I, while working on the development of the approach, lived in Russia, which simply could not be reflected in this book.

Therefore, it is important to note that most of the examples in the book use the Russian ruble as currency when specifying values. And this should in no way mislead the reader because I would like the examples to be understood simply as figures. The important thing is how these numbers relate to each other; the absolute value is irrelevant. In the future, I will most likely develop new examples that will be closest to the idea of the Western reader who is used to the euro or dollar.

In any case, I believe that the methodology described in the book will be useful to the reader, as it makes it easy to get the answers that entrepreneurs face at the beginning of their thorny path in building a successful business.

I will also be grateful for any feedback and am ready to answer questions on the methodology described in the book at daniil@khanin.info. You can also send any comments on this publication, errors, and inaccuracies found.

Sincerely,
Daniil Khanin
Barcelona, Spain
12.02.2024

Introduction

What is this book about?

Quite a lot of people have been facing lately the challenge of making their business effective. They wonder how to make money from the ideas they are trying to implement? At the same time, it is desirable for them to attract investments to implement these ideas. It is not clear for such people how to find a better solution for these challenges.

The era of easy money, when investors were not particularly interested in getting into specifics of the project, has come to an end. Investors all over the world began not only to monitor the investment prospects and innovativeness of the projects, but also to carefully study their financial models in order to determine realistic forecasts for achieving profitability.

On the one hand, you can hire professional experts in the field of financial planning who can create a proper financial plan for the project, describe all the parameters and help defend it when talking to the investor. However, in the first place, the services of such specialists are expensive and they are usually busy working in large companies. As a rule, they do not have any free time left to work on a startup, even a promising one. In the second place, modern innovative startups are launched in very harsh conditions of total uncertainty, which generally limits the work of professional financiers who are accustomed to working with access to huge volumes of market information.

I wasn't the only one contemplating this issue: back in the early 2000s, American venture capitalist David Skok was looking for a tool for a simple and quick assessment of startups. He understood that the financial models prepared by the startup owners, though created to explain the prospects of the project, did not stand up to close examination. He decided to assess startups using unit economics, an approach taken from classic business management economics, in which he proposed to change the scaling unit, moving it from product to customer.

So, in this book, I will try to explain how unit economics can help an innovative startup entrepreneur to manage innovative projects.

We will gradually explore what tasks an entrepreneur faces and how they can be digitized. We will also learn why such digitalization is important, and how unit economics emerges. We will observe the transition of the scaling unit from "product" that was initially used to assess production tasks to "client" that is currently the standard for innovative enterprises and is slowly penetrating into classic business management.

We will analyze an example of creation of new business models based on the results of the unit economics approach showing the impossibility of achieving the business characteristics set within the original business model, and how and why it had to be changed.

We will find out how the unit economics works in general for different types of business models, such as classic model, a basic or simple unit economics model that can be applied to approximately 95% of startups, and for mixed models used when it comes to social media business models, lead generation models, marketplaces, etc.

In the following chapters, I will address the issue of decision making in business: what should be done if the unit economics of the business does not add up or the current situation in the company prevents it from being profitable. We will pay attention to such topics as finding growth points, creating a focus strategy for startups and prioritizing tasks. To do this, we will briefly get acquainted with Goldratt's theory of constraints that has the key to finding answers to these questions using unit economics.

Particular attention will be paid to cohort analysis. The point is that the people responsible for creating the products work with the needs of clients, while the existing financial instruments deal with time periods: a month, a quarter, a year. This causes the difference in understanding of values between an entrepreneur and a financial expert. The former analyses the customer's value within the possibility of a lifetime value (LTV) and is ready to sacrifice the profit from the first sales in favor of the future loyalty, while the latter simply analyzes data within selected periods of time and records profit and loss.

Cohorts are a very important and flexible tool for evaluation of your target audience. It also helps making important management decisions aimed at attracting clients, meeting their needs and earning money over a long period of time. I will explain how the cohorts are formed, dwell on the questions about the way time is structured within them, and teach you how to calculate the main characteristics of the product and the customer, such as LTV, in cohorts.

And finally, we will find out how to reconcile financiers with product development managers and to combine unit economics – a decision-making tool for a product developer – with financial documents to which the financial officers are accustomed. We will consider a unique approach to developing a financial model created based on the team's expertise, rather than delusions about the product and the market, as it was common a few years ago.

Particular attention will be paid to such questions as how to calculate investments for a startup, to take account of the various stages of investment, to build a Cap table for investors and to allocate shares correctly. And, most importantly, how to be able to defend your financial plan when presented to the investor.

Who is this book for?

The book will be useful primarily for those who want to find out more about a technique that allows one to make data driven decisions in business, to understand that business is done for earning money and to learn how the team's actions can lead to earning this very money.

You might be launching your very first startup and looking for the tips on how to make fewer mistakes. Or you are already an experienced entrepreneur who, on the contrary, has made many mistakes and suffered a large number of failures in managing business projects, and you are looking for new knowledge that will aid you in your new endeavors. You also might be a product owner at a large corporation and want to understand how your management would evaluate your work. Perhaps, you are an investor who is trying to figure out what is the best way to evaluate startups and understand the likelihood of them achieving their stated goals.

In all these cases, this book will be useful for you as it was written by an entrepreneur for entrepreneurs and accumulates extensive experience, more than 20 years of launching projects, as well as building financial models and defining unit economics as a decision-making tool in business.

Why me?

In 1986, my older brother took me to a gaming club in the suburbs of Irkutsk where we lived then. There, for the first time in my life I saw a computer, an Atari 65XE, and played a game, River Raid. Back then, I couldn't imagine that my whole life would be connected with computers, but that's exactly what happened.

Then, the year 1988 came bringing in my life the "Young Technician" magazine that published a PC assembly diagram. And in 1990, thanks to the combined efforts of my brother and father, the first computer appeared at our house and I became absorbed in programming. I also remember a magazine my father brought from the exhibition "Informatics in Life of the USA[1]". I read this edition so many times I could recite the text. I was particularly impressed by the article about computer networks and the opportunities they presented.

In 1995, I managed to gain access to the Internet through the international project aimed at exploring earthquakes, as I was indirectly involved in this project. And in 1997, I began to work closely with this network.

In 1998, I was engaged in online advertising. It was not yet a business, but it was already the beginning of the long journey that I eventually took prior to writing this book.

In 2005, having completed my PhD research at the Russian Academy of Sciences, I decided to launch the region's first online advertising agency. From that moment on, I was engaged exclusively in innovative IT business. I managed to build the largest online advertising holding in

---

[1] "Informatics in Life of the USA" is an American exhibition that took place in major cities of the USSR in 1987-1988. The exhibition demonstrated the latest US achievements in the field of computing, communications and telecommunications.

the Tomsk region (federal subject of Russia in the southwest of the Siberian Federal District), that I quite successfully sold in 2018. I launched the largest conference dedicated to the Internet business and IT technologies, which still exists and is known as "Gorod.IT".

However, I also had unsuccessful projects, such as the service for ordering a taxi through a mobile application that enabled the user to call a taxi using coordinates on the map. I was developing the project in 2008 and this is the time when Uber appeared on the market, if I am not mistaken. The service had no chance even to be released, but it was fun.

To launch it, I had to develop my own mapping service and draw my own maps, since at that time there was simply not a single map of Tomsk on the Internet.

But all these projects did not last long, the maps soon covered the whole world, "Yandex.Taxi" beat all competitors in Russia, and my project went on the shelf as an example of the fact that not all business endeavors are successful.

My key achievement was the launch of a service for selling advertising on the Internet in the Tomsk region. It was aimed at showing advertising to people who are most likely to be interested in it. It was possible to describe the target audience using dozens of parameters. The advertiser paid only for real contacts of network users with the advertising medium. We also provided reports on the advertising efficiency. All this was developed in 2008–2010, and we were pretty much the pioneers of targeted online advertising in Russia. Moreover, some of our technologies became unique and innovative in the world, but I did not know or understand it then.

At this time, I met a person who had a great influence on me and my understanding of the business activities I performed. In particular, he helped me develop the products that formed the basis of this book. I met Gleb Tertychny, an evangelist of Goldratt's Theory of Constraints. He explained to me how it can be applied to information technologies, and showed that the conveyor system does not have to be material – it can also be metaphorical. This idea later formed the basis for the search for growth points in unit economics.

In 2012, I met Nick Mikhailovsky, who invited me to move to Moscow in order to develop a revolutionary new approach to the market of e-commerce marketing together. We launched one of the first personalization services for online stores in Russia – Crossss. It offered the best in the world technologies that were ahead of any global solutions emerging at the moment. But back then I did not have enough experience and simply did not know how to run a business in conditions of super-tough and aggressive competition. Moreover, at that time I knew nothing about startups and had never heard about them, though my business was exactly one of them.

As a result, in 2014, I sold the company and found myself in a situation in which I gained very useful experience and knowledge, had time and opportunities to do something else, and was invited to work with startups at the largest venture fund in Europe – IIDF.

Working at the fund, I was involved in several things: communication with startup teams (later on a new profession would arise and such specialists would be called business trackers), primary selection and analysis of financial models of startups. So, looking through the applications of startup teams and their models and communicating with the founders, I faced the understanding that not one of the thousands – and I actually looked through several thousand financial models over the years – entrepreneurs could clearly describe and explain to me the financial model that was submitted as part of an application. The figures were entered into the table according to a template and had no basis. Many of the applicants did not even know what parameters these numbers showed.

At IIDF, I met Ilya Krasinsky, who said that the effectiveness of product development can be assessed in the same way as I assessed the effectiveness of advertising. Thanks to him, I learned about the Data Driven approach and unit economics. I finally realized what exactly I had been doing all this time.

In 2015, I noticed that startups were constantly calculating their unit economics, but were having a lot of trouble writing down simple formulas. And I decided to launch ueCalc.com.

At first, it was a very simple service located on a blog. It allowed startup owners to calculate their economics without using Excel. A little later, I added the ability to search for growth points and designed this program into a separate product.

However, when interviewing startup developers, I could not understand why they were unable to explain their financial model, if they had all the figures that they produce and include into unit economics.

Closer to 2020, I finally came up with a mechanism that would allow the user to automatically create a financial plan for income and expenses knowing the unit economics of the product. And since then, in addition to its other functions, ueCalc.com has been able to create such plans. The main advantage of the approach is that the entrepreneur focuses specifically on his team and his product, as he knows best how to satisfy the needs of his customers. The financial planning is taken care of by the calculator, and you can build a financial model based solely on the team's competencies.

All this took quite a long time to be developed, and I managed to travel all over Russia – from Vladivostok to Kaliningrad and from Murmansk and Norilsk to Grozny, telling entrepreneurs about my ideas. In total, I presented my approach and performed as a speaker more than 300 times and was eventually invited to the Lomonosov Moscow State University Business School to turn my knowledge into a semester-long course on Unit Economics.

During my presentations, I regularly received a question whether it was possible to read something on the topic of unit economics, and this question puzzled me. On the one hand, there is the blog of David Skok[2], whom I consider to be the author of this approach. But David doesn't write much about unit economics focusing mainly on the venture industry. If he mentions unit economics, it is within the framework of SaaS, that he is involved in as an investor. Next, I

---

[2] https://www.forentrepreneurs.com/

thought about Ilya Krasinsky, who at the time of writing this book ran a Telegram channel[3], but the posts did not appear regularly. Oleg Yakubenkov also wrote on this topic in his blog GoPractice.ru. As a result, he turned the blog into one of the best simulators for product managers. But at the same time, there is nowhere a single place that concentrates information about what unit economics is, how to use it, how to look for answers and what conclusions can be drawn from these calculations. I do not know of a single book on this topic that would be of interest and that I could recommend to my audience.

As a result, I thought about writing my own and began collecting information, writing various articles, recording videos and publishing them on my channel[4]. To write this book, I had to rebuild all my material from scratch, conduct a deep fact-check, try to understand why this approach had not been developed earlier and how it happened that it was actually being fundamentally developed from Russia.

---

[3] https://t.me/ilya_krasinsky

[4] https://youtube.com/c/datadrivendecisions

What is unit economics?

Responsibilities of an entrepreneur

Prior to trying to find the answers to the questions about the tasks that can be covered by unit economics, it is essential to understand the tasks that a business founder must perform and take into account. After all, one must remember that unit economics is only a tool of the entrepreneur.

At the very beginning of his business journey, an entrepreneur wants to be sure that his idea will work and bring profit. Of course, new entrepreneurs often experience excitement and an adrenaline rush that prevents them from thinking critically about their ideas. However, anyone who has started his own business has an idea of the expected profit.

Many of you may remember how passionately you felt about a new idea and spoke about the way this idea would help you make a lot of money. First – to friends and colleagues, then, when the belief in your success grew stronger, –

to investors in order to receive funding for your project.

However, not everyone manages to captivate even the colleagues with the idea, not to mention investors. Friends, and especially capitalists, ask a bunch of questions that usually have no answers. Some of them are left out as they were not even considered on the stage of developing the project. The investor wants to know how much money the participation in your project will bring him, how the business will develop, how it will grow. He is interested in the sum that is required to be invested, the period of investment and what the money will be used for. Do the company's expenses correspond to the income declared in the project? And a huge number of other questions that are usually associated with numbers and that the entrepreneur has not thought about.

To answer these questions, the author of the idea begins to prepare a financial model – a profit and loss statement. Moreover, in most cases, he does not have his own experience in creating such a document. This also makes it difficult to involve external specialists to the creation of the document, since it is quite hard to check their work without knowledge of how this document should be structured, what certain values in it depend on, and what exactly the investor wants to see.

As a result, the entrepreneur spends a lot of effort to actually invent the document and adjust it to the investor's expectations. However, many figures contradict each other. For example, according to the document, one manager is required to work with each of 20 clients. In the end of the plan, the number of clients is declared to be 2000, while the salary is included only for 10 managers, who must be accommodated in an office of 20 m² along with the remaining 30 employees.

It also raises questions about the reason the number of clients should grow by leaps and bounds and the basis on which the growth step was chosen. Such documents are a torture for both the entrepreneurs, who exhaust themselves while creating them, and investors, who do not understand how they should ultimately evaluate the project, so they simply refuse to invest.

Filling out the plan is especially challenging for entrepreneurs who work with innovative products, since they simply do not have any possibility to obtain the data required to be included into the document, as well as demonstrate how this data will change over time. The innovation project developer is in a situation of complete uncertainty.

With experience, emotions fade into the background, and the project developer wonders more and more whether it is possible to somehow test his idea for potential success.

After the project has already been launched and the first investments have been attracted, the entrepreneur faces new challenges, usually related to the fact that the reality does not correspond to the plans. Fewer clients are being attracted, expenses exceed estimates, and the funds disappear faster than initially expected.

Apart from the question of how to save the business, it is necessary to understand why it is not possible to fulfill the plan and what indicators need to be improved first taking into account the available resources. It would also be beneficial to determine what changes should be made in the business process to allow you to improve the situation and begin to implement the plan. At the same time, it is important to understand that all these questions arise in a critical situation when the entrepreneur is limited in time and resources, and also lacks data.

When you manage to stabilize the business and reach a minimal degree of certainty, it is necessary to focus on such tasks as monitoring the efficiency of workers, hiring staff and making sure they are concentrated on producing the result. How to evaluate the performance of an employee? What to pay attention to? What benefits does this employee bring to the business by performing his tasks?

Imagine that the team gathers for a weekly planning meeting. They discuss tasks, agree on plans and begin to implement them. A week later, at a new planning meeting, you see that some of these tasks were performed, some had to be postponed or replaced with others, and some were completed with negative results. The discussion takes place, new tasks are formulated on the results, and the team starts working. Such a situation may occur again and again for quite a long time and the entrepreneur will constantly be speculating on how this can affect the success of his business.

It is no secret that in large companies there are always employees who are good at imitating vigorous activity while producing no visible results. However, according to formal criteria, they do perform their work well.

However, no business can exist indefinitely without the opportunity to develop and increase profit. Therefore, even large successful companies eventually reduce their staff. Others do not survive the battle with time and go bankrupt.

All these situations only make the company owner more stressed out and prevent him from concentrating on his project. It would be nice to have a tool that helps you to find answers to all these questions easily and to have at your disposal the financial documents that are quickly produced and easy-to-understand both for yourself and for the investors. One of such tools is unit economics.

Unit economics, along with other methods and approaches that will be discussed in this book, allows us to answer the questions raised above. At the same time, its main task is to make sure that the entrepreneur spends less time on this process and uses the minimum set of data that he can actually obtain, control and understand.

So, unit economics helps assess the prospects of the project, estimate how successful it can be and what kind of income to expect. It allows one to easily create a financial document in which the entrepreneur will know his way around, understand every figure and, therefore, know how to talk to the investor, how much investment to ask for and for how long. In general, he will be able to answer any question related to the matter. As it was mentioned before, minimum information is necessary in order to create such a document. Mainly, the information regarding the idea itself and the team that will implement this idea.

Unit economics is also a useful tool for managing the work of employees, it helps formulate tasks and provides focus in business. With this approach, you no longer have to rack your brains with assessing the team's effectiveness in completing tasks: this tool shows very clearly who is working on the tasks and who isn't and how effectively it is done. And most importantly, it helps demonstrate how much the implementation of these tasks bring the entire business closer to success.

Of course, it is important to understand that unit economics is not a silver bullet that will solve all the problems of an entrepreneur. But at least, it provides an opportunity to get answers to specific questions and leave more time for creativity in business.

The introduction of steam machines into manufacturing of textiles

A certain John Peel, 35 years old, returning on April 15, 1800, to Cromford, his native town, after military service in India, realized that he, in fact, had nothing to do. So, he decided to found a modern production – a weaving factory. He knew that James Watt had developed a steam engine which meant that the fabric could be produced on an industrial scale. Peel found this innovation quite interesting, and he contemplated the idea of opening a factory.

To fulfill his idea, Peel needed to find premises, negotiate the acquisition of machinery for the new enterprise with the manufacturer, discuss the terms of wool supply for the fabric, find a market (textile sellers), discuss the conditions of cooperation and hire people. Of course, this is an approximate list of tasks that John Peel needed to manage in order to launch a business, but these are the most basic ones.

Before launching his business, John decided to evaluate the prospects of his ideas in order to be sure of future success. He certainly believed in the future of steam engines, but he did not have much wealth and knew that he would need to attract investments, which meant he had to be sure that he was not making a mistake.

Peel negotiated the supply of five machines with Watt's company. The total cost of the machines was £5,000 and it was a huge sum for that time. He found a suitable building that could accommodate production and a small warehouse, the purchase of which would cost him £2,500. All that was left to do was to find wool, people and, most importantly, money.

To resolve this issue, Peel turned to a local bank to obtain a loan. According to estimates, he needed to get about 10,000 pounds of credit in order to pay for the machines, the building, purchase materials for the first six months of work, and also have enough money to pay the wages to his 25 employees.

After lengthy negotiations with bankers and a personal recommendation from Mr. Watt, Peel's application to receive money for launching his production was approved. Everything was in place – the plan, the innovation, the funding for the project, and John began to implement his idea.

7 months later, by the end of 1800, Peel's factory launched the production of fabric in rolls. Watt's modern machines made it possible to produce textiles of better quality, in larger volumes and with lower price, which meant the number of

buyers could increase significantly. The business raised expectations for success.

A couple of months before the opening, Peel decided to calculate how many rolls of fabric he needed to produce and sell per month in order to be able to regularly pay down his loan, pay wages, purchase materials and coal for Watt's machines, and earn money for his old age. To do this, he determined that he wanted to become not just a successful businessman, but also a rich man. Therefore, earning a fabulous 100 pounds a month did not seem unattainable to him.

To earn £100, Peel must have covered all his regular expenses arising while running the business. What did they include? John reasoned this way:

- Loan repayment
- Wages of employees
- Payment for energy (purchase of coal for a steam engine)
- Purchase of raw materials
- Product advertising

Mr. Peel incurred some of these expenses constantly, even if there were no sales, and some were incurred only when there were clients. For example, he could purchase materials only if he received an order for production. Whereas, he must have paid down the loan even if there were no sales. The same thing with wages, payment for energy for the factory, etc.

We call the former expenses that do not occur when there are no customers "variable", and the later expenses that we have to cover even if there are no sales, "fixed".

It is important to understand that the term "fixed expenses" means that such expenses we cover throughout the operation of the business on a regular basis. And they are not necessarily fixed over time. We will see later that fixed expenses can be, and often are, dynamic.

Having performed lengthy calculations, Peel realized that his monthly fixed expenses would be £1,750. Then, he needed to figure out how much textile he must produce in order to earn £1,750 needed to cover his fixed expenses and £100 over it for himself.

Mr. John Peel decided to sell a unit of production (a roll of fabric) for 10 pounds. At the same time, the cost of raw materials was only 20% of the price, which meant it was possible to earn 8 pounds from each roll of fabric sold. The difference between the cost of a product and the cost of its production is called gross profit.

In order to sell his textiles, Mr. Peel planned to attract the customers by placing advertisements in a newspaper that had recently begun its operation in the city. Customer acquisition costs are taken from gross profit. If we divide all monthly customer acquisition costs by the number of rolls sold, we get 0.5 pounds. The difference between gross profit and acquisition costs is called contribution margin (Contribution Margin = Gross Profit – Acquisition costs). Thus, Mr. Peel expected to earn £7.5 in contribution margin by selling one roll of fabric.

And now, Peel could calculate how many rolls of textile he should produce and sell per month. In order to do this, he needs all the fixed expenses (1,750 pounds and 100 pounds for himself), that is 1,850 pounds, divide by the contribution margin received from one roll – 7.5 pounds.

$(1750 + 100) / 7.5 = 246.6(6)$

Thus, 247 rolls of fabric needed to be produced and sold per month.

It was necessary to discuss the sales with fabric sellers in the city, and better yet, in the neighboring cities and even in London, thereby assessing the current demand in order to make sure that such a volume of fabric could be sold. In addition to this research, Peel believed that by offering textiles at a lower price than his competitors, who produced it by hand, he could reach a wider segment of the population and further increase sales of the product.

Having carried out all the calculations, Peel was confident that he could cover all the expenses for his idea, and opened the factory in 1801. Over the years, he earned a good fortune and was able to leave it to his children along with factories that were already operating in several cities of England.

Even though this story is fictitious, this is exactly what unit economics looked like until the end of the 20th century. It answered the main question – how much products need to be produced and sold in order to cover fixed expenses and earn the necessary profit. However, at the end of the 20th century, the dot-com crash occurred, and this changed unit economics beyond recognition.

Dot-com bubble collapse

The approach to using unit economics and managing business in general in the 20th century was no different from what Peel did in the 19th century. However, some changes in business still took place. The investors were the first ones to realize that the computer industry that was emerging in the early 70s offered enormous opportunities for making money. Different companies grew by leaps and bounds and brought huge profits. For example, it is known that Warren Buffett, having met Bill Gates in the 80s, bought shares of Microsoft and earned $37 billion.

Therefore, since the 80s, a huge number of investors paid close attention to what was happening in this new industry: the advent of personal computers, the battle between Microsoft and Apple, etc. Everyone wanted to see the new gold mine.

So, at the end of 1989, an English scientist working at CERN, Timothy Berners-Lee, proposed a project that implied organizing information, publishing hyper documents that were interconnected by hyperlinks – in fact, he came up with the Internet in its modern form, or the World Wide Web.

Berners-Lee's creation of such technologies and innovations as a web server, a web browser with the possibility to quickly create web pages, simply blew up the minds of people of the whole world. Internet projects began to appear en masse. On August 6, 1991, Timothy Berners-Lee published the world's first website online. In fact, I first went online and visited a website in 1995, just four years after the Internet appeared in its current form.

Investors observed these changes, no longer wanting to miss out on profit. They began to invest en masse in new technology companies that started to appear due to the minimum entry threshold. At the same time, many investors have lost sight of the fact that for such companies the presence of the Internet was only a tool for conducting real business processes. For example, at this time the current industry giant Amazon appeared. Initially, it was only a store that received orders via the Internet, but at the same time it carried out its activities in the real world and had full-fledged business processes.

However, many companies simply created websites that were used by other people – for example, in order to build their own websites – earning no money at all. At the same time, manufacturers of telecommunication equipment, such as Cisco, Nortel and others, began to invest in production capacities, suggesting that soon the demand for their products will increase significantly.

All these and many other factors, that are mentioned in various sources and are still easy to find on the Internet[5, 6], led to the fact that venture investors began to invest in any company that somehow connected itself with the Internet. Venture capitalists have been joined by young millionaires from tech companies who became

---

[5] https://www.cnet.com/tech/computing/the-greatest-defunct-websites-and-dotcom-disasters/

[6] https://www.salon.com/2000/04/25/party_5/

millionaires through IPOs. They knew that Internet companies were made by engineers and programmers just like them, and they believed that they would be successful.

At the same time, Internet companies spent huge amounts of money on advertising and considered it necessary to increase their audience first, and only then earn profit for shareholders. Sometimes this led to absurd situations: the company threw a party devoted to the launching of a website[7]. Advertising expenses have become simply crazy: while only two Internet companies bought advertising for the 33rd Super Bowl, the largest sports show in the United States, it was already 17 out of 61 advertisers for the 34th Super Bowl (some sources indicate from 12 to19 Internet companies, depending on what is considered a dot-com).

---

[7] https://www.latimes.com/archives/la-xpm-2000-dec-25-mn-4559-story.html

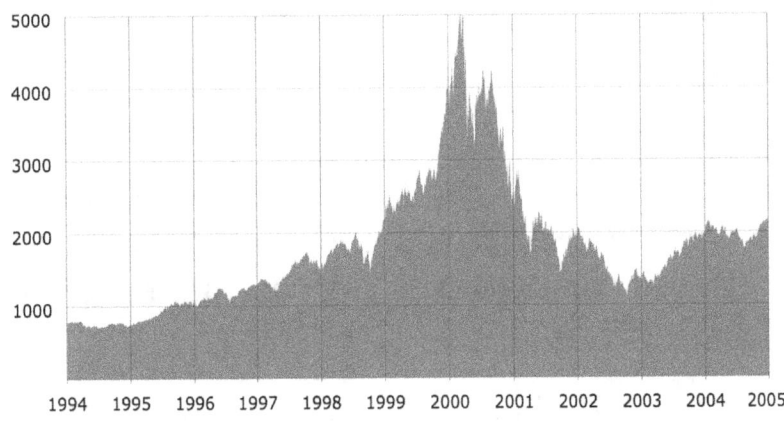

On March 10, 2000, the NASDAQ index reached its maximum — 5048.62 — and then collapsed. Moreover, while the NASDAQ was losing its positions, the S&P500 was growing, which meant that investors were disappointed in Internet companies and began to withdraw funds in order to invest into a traditional business that was understandable to them.

The real point of interest here is not only that the collapse of dot-coms led to a fall in the market and declined interest in Internet companies, but the fact that, like any crisis, it cleaned the market removing bad players and weak firms. A huge

---

[8] https://en.wikipedia.org/wiki/Dot-com_bubble

number of companies went bankrupt, many lost the lion's share of capitalization.

However, the best ones survived – those with liquidity, those who managed to maintain investor's faith or profits, and some of them, such as Google or Amazon, are current leaders in global business.

But the main thing that made me mention this period in this book was the emergence and development of a popular new business model, namely Soft as a Service, or SaaS: subscription software. The surviving Internet companies were looking for opportunities to make money from their users in every possible way.

And while the existing giants, such as Microsoft, Norton, Adobe and others, sold software at high prices and in boxes, the new companies faced a problem: they could not sell any boxes, their software consisted of a website and there was exactly one copy. The users went to the website and got access to the product from anywhere in the world at the same time. Then, it was decided to sell access to the product by subscription, a small amount of money per month for the right to use it. Back then it became a revolution, but now it is the norm, and we gladly pay for many subscriptions to various software. For example, online cinemas, which give access to a huge number of films for the price of two tickets to the cinema.

However, the new model, though successful and attractive to many people, also gave rise to new problems — it became difficult for companies to understand how much product they need to sell in order to cover production expenses. In fact, the textile manufacture faced the same issue, but instead of steam engines there were prog-rammers. And if the existing giants could easily calculate how many boxes with software they needed to produce in order to bring the required profit to investors, then Internet companies produced a single product and just gave the right to use it to a huge audience for a small fee.

In addition, the understanding of the key process in business changed, and instead of selling products the way Peel did, Internet companies came to buying customers. The fact is that the Internet made it possible to work with the whole world at once, and the growing number of companies meant enormous competition for the audience. Crazy amounts of money were spent on attracting one client. We remember that this was one of the reasons for the collapse of the dot-coms — the expenses on them were not covered by a one-time subscription payment. But the beauty of the subscription model was that customers, having subscribed, paid not just once, but a lot. This means that by estimating the average number of payments received from one client, it is possible to estimate the costs of attracting him – which means spending more money on this than Peel could afford in the 19th century.

This transition from the sale of goods to the purchase of a client led to a revision of the unit economics itself. The calculation of contribution margin began to be based on the client, and not on the unit of production. On the one hand, the tool became more advanced, it made it possible to realistically evaluate the effectiveness of advertising campaigns. But at the same time, it gave rise to many new difficulties - for example, entrepreneurs now had to dive into cohort analysis in order to correctly calculate unit economics.

Just like this, one financial crisis caused a change in unit economics and allowed new companies to use old principles in new ways for their new business models. On the pages of this book, we will see once again how another crisis led to the emergence of new approaches to management, which, together with unit economics, allowed entrepreneurs to answer a lot of questions that we mentioned at the beginning of this chapter.

David Skok

One of the first people to begin transferring unit economics from the world of manufacturing to the world of Internet companies was the legend of the global venture industry, David Skok, General Partner of one of the most successful venture funds in the world - Matrix Capital. David specializes in SaaS investments, and in his line of work, he has had to evaluate a huge number of applications from various Internet companies using the SaaS monetization model. At the same time, after the dot-com collapse, investors began to treat startups more carefully and also check their business plans more thoroughly. And this became a problem. The standard document describing the prospects of a business was the P&L plan. The entrepreneur would provide the investor with such a plan in order to justify the required investment and explain how the new company planned to spend and earn money.

At the same time, innovative entrepreneurs could not properly fill out such a plan due to insufficient knowledge about the market, and often simply due to the lack of any information, given the uniqueness of the new technology. And this was generally normal for innovations; even Akio Morita, the founder of Sony, talking in his book[9] about the creation of the first portable audio player, the Walkman, said that it is impossible to study user's interest in a product if people have no idea it exists. Thus, any marketing research in the innovation area is complicated, and there is simply nowhere to get the data to fill out the P&L. But investors were cautious and demanded such a document, since for them it was an important tool for assessing the business.

At the same time, David understood that it was simply unrealistic for an entrepreneur of an innovative business who is using an innovative subscription monetization model to create such a document. Such entrepreneurs lacked both knowledge and information. Still, entrepreneurs make such documents and adjust them to the interests and demands of the investor. As a result, instead of a useful document, all participants receive a useless document that does

---

[9] Sony. Made in Japan.

not help, but makes things worse. And then, he wondered if it was possible to obtain insight and information about the business that would be considered the most reliable in order to conclude whether the entrepreneur could achieve these indicators, and based on these parameters, make investment decisions.

As a result, he came up with two simple indicators that he began to use as the basis for the initial assessment of startups: LTV[10] and CAC. Just think about it: instead of a huge document that sometimes contains hundreds of parameters and tens of thousands of cells, David began to rely on just two, which, in his opinion, describe the business quite representatively.

What are these parameters? LTV, or, as I will refer to it further on, CLTV, is the gross profit that a client brings for the entire time that we consider him a client. We will pay close attention to this time period later. And CAC is the sum of the marketing expenses aimed at attracting this customer to the business. These two parameters

---

[10] Later on, I will use the term CLTV to clearly emphasize that we are talking specifically about the customer's lifetime gross profit, since further on I will separate CLTV and LTV.

are enough to make the calculation of cont-ribution margin that Peel made to assess the prospects of his business in the 19th century. But why CLTV and not Gross Profit?

Previously, gross profit was calculated per unit of production, and this product was sold only once. Therefore, having a final price of the product along with the costs of its production and sto-rage, we could easily obtain the gross profit value. In SaaS, a client, having been attracted once, pays for the product again and again over a long period of time. Therefore, the same client brings money in different periods of time, but in general, we attract him only once.

In fact, CLTV is the sum of gross profit from all the payments a customer will make. We will look at the formulas for calculating metrics in more detail in the following chapters. In the meantime, let's figure out why these two metrics were enough for David to understand whether it was worth investing in a business or not.

Definition of unit economics

To better understand the mechanisms of making profit in a company, let's look at one example. Using small rectangles, I will demonstrate how finances work in business.

The first rectangle is revenue (or turnover): all the money a business receives from the sale of goods and services. We are now considering a situation of one sale to one client, which means that in this case the revenue will be equal to the average check.

Revenue

But, as a famous Soviet cartoon character Uncle Fedya always said, in order to sell something you do not need, you must buy something you do not need first. Therefore, we need to spend money in order to gain a certain object we are going to sell. In economics, this is called a prime cost, or Cost of Good Sold, abbreviated as COGS.

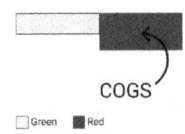

COGS

Green Red

To picture it, I have drawn a red rectangle. Note that it is higher than the revenue (green rectangle). This is a very strange example, that actually shows that we are selling a product or service here at a lower price than the one we paid in order to acquire this product or service. This is a visualization of the famous joke: I sell a dollar for 90 cents. I didn't count the profit, but the turnover is huge.

Of course, we can't do this, because we will go bankrupt simply because we do have sales. But I took this example on purpose, as I have seen such a situation in many startups. In many cases, the teams simply don't understand economics. Such cases sometimes can also be controlled: for example, when a business plans to capture the market using the volume of transactions and subsidizes such transactions compensating for the difference. Typically, such expenses are written off for marketing and have clear boundaries: how much the business is willing to spend, how long the subsidization will last, and so on.

In general, your actions should be aimed at your COGS being less than the average check.

Then we have a difference between the average check and COGS that is called a Gross Profit.

Gross profit is the first and quite important profit in business. It shows how effective the transaction is. So that we do not sell a product for a lesser price than the one we paid to buy it.

Then, we move to the next stage. In order to sell something you do not need, it is not enough just to buy something you do not need — you also need to find someone who will buy this something. It means, you need to spend money to attract a client.

Again, I drew a red rectangle that is higher than the gross profit. This means that the acquisition

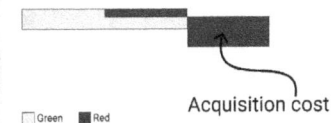

Acquisition cost

costs may exceed the gross profit earned from one transaction with this client. Therefore, the business expects that this client will return and make a second, third and subsequent purchases, and we will not have any expenses for his return, and that in fact does not always happen.

I demonstrate this option because it often takes place in modern business, especially in highly competitive areas. We will consider the case in which the acquisition costs are less than the gross profit from one transaction. But, again, I am giving this example now only to demonstrate how business economics works.

Now, it is clearly visible that we have a balance of

funds. If we subtract the acquisition costs from the gross profit, we get the Contribution Margin. In a modern product approach to business, this type of profit is a quite important one.

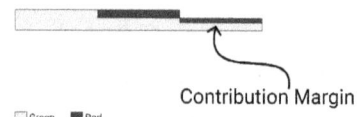

Contribution Margin

☐ Green ■ Red

So, we bought something we do not need and even found someone who would buy this something. Have we taken everything into account or is there anything else that needs to be included in the calculations?

Indeed, for our business to function, we must spend money on rent, employee salaries, and the like. These are the so-called fixed costs.

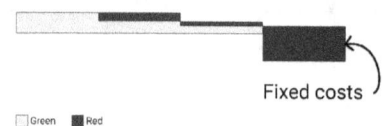

Fixed costs

☐ Green ■ Red

It is clear that in most cases the cost of running a business will exceed the contribution margin from one sale to one client. Therefore, for a business to exist, it is necessary to somehow cover the difference between fixed costs and contribution margin.

Required investments

Green ■ Red

In general, I call this the required investment. Moreover, I mean the investments in the broad sense of the word: it can be venture investments, a bank loan, or personal funds of the founders. In any case, the business must have money to survive.

So, we have looked at the basic concepts related to business economics and the way they relate to each other. Now it's time to finally figure out what unit economics is.

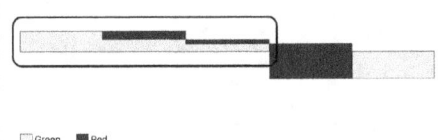

Green ■ Red

The area outlined in blue is what I call one unit — the same unit that is used in the name of the methodology, unit economics. Essentially, this is the economics of one transaction. Further, we will consider other options. Moreover, the technique will work better with other application options, but for now this does not matter. So, let us assume that our unit is a single sale to one client. And, as you can see, such sales will not be enough to cover fixed costs, so the business requires investments.

What happens if we make one more deal?

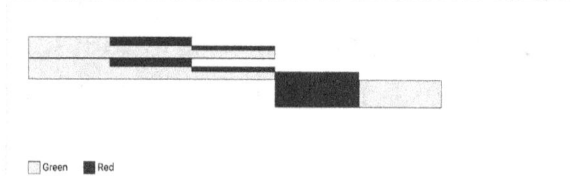

For ease of perception, let's add up the similar entities: checks, expenses, acquisition costs, and so on.

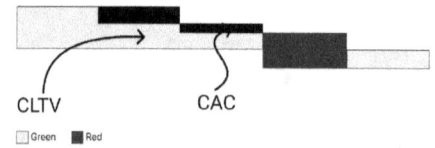

Note that the required investment has decreased since the contribution margin from two units is greater than from one.

Now we make three units.

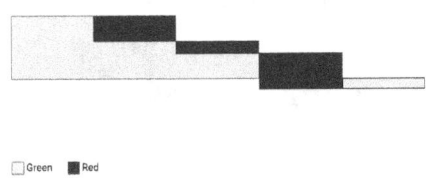

Then, four units.

It is clearly seen that almost all fixed costs are already covered by contribution margin. And finally, five units.

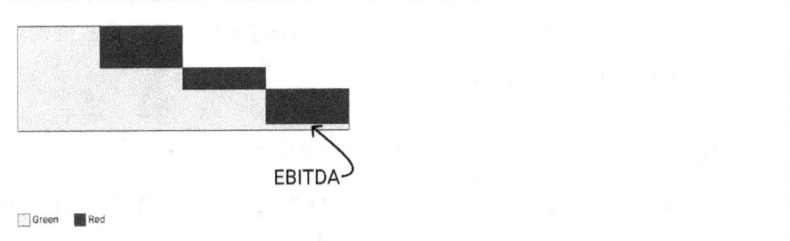

EBITDA

The contribution margin from five units covered the fixed costs completely, and we see the difference that for now I will simply call the profit, but actually it is the EBITDA (Earnings before interest, tax, amortization and depreciation). However, now we need to pay attention to three parts of the big picture: fixed costs, profit and the contribution margin.

What do these three entities tell us? Here's what: in order for a business to reach the required level of profit, having given fixed costs, we need to get a certain contribution margin from all the scaling units.

Now we can define unit economics. Unit economics is the process of determining the number of scaling units, the contribution margin from which is necessary to cover fixed costs and reach a given level of profit.

In fact, David Skok proposed to evaluate business prospects using unit economics, in which he replaced gross profit with the gross profit from all transactions of the client, calling it CLTV. He reasoned, if a startup can extract contribution margin from its activities but at the same time has losses due to fixed costs, then, by increasing the number of scaling units, such a business can pass the break-even point with a sufficient market (in the following chapters I will show how all of it can be calculated) and start making profit. At the same time, the two metrics that David used are quite easy for a startup to obtain and pass on to an investor for analysis. Obviously, this is much easier than creating a complex financial document that contains a lot of parameters and a huge amount of data, sometimes taken from nowhere. Further in the book, I will explain how you can create a P&L plan relying solely on unit economics and simple knowledge of mathematics.

Business model

Unit economics for simple monetization models

It's time to learn how the product is perceived within the unit economics and how it helps the developer working with the product. In this chapter, I will dwell on the way it describes different monetization models and what special features should be considered when choosing these very models.

To begin with, let's imagine the product as a process the input of which is an action that leads to the appearance of customers for this product and the output is money. Now, we will discuss mainly gross and marginal types of profit. That is, our diagram should demonstrate how the product can make money by serving customers.

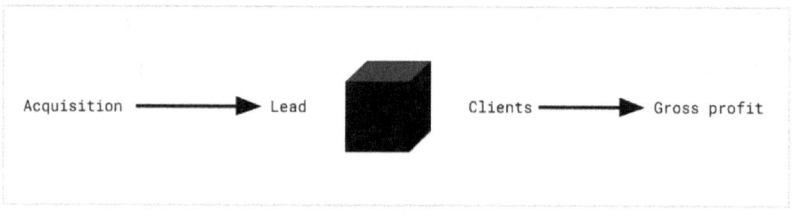

Let's take a closer look at this process: at the input we have an action that I called attracting. It is responsible for attracting the attention of potential customers. Indeed, the potential ones, not those who paid for the product. Next, potential customers interact with the black box that symbolizes the product itself. I call it "a black box" because no one knows what's going on inside except the person who develops it. But the main thing is that the output is the customers who bring us gross profit.

Why does this diagram show us potential clients, and not the real ones? This is actually very important for all our future work. This is an artificial method that will be required more than once in this book. And it will slightly change David Skok's approach to unit economics.

As an example, let's consider a manager working in a certain company who is responsible for attracting an audience to some project. Let us name him John. Our John's tasks include launching advertising campaigns to attract customers to the business. At the same time, his work is evaluated by the result, namely by the number of clients he attracted. The business owner set these rules because he believes that managing a business based on data is the right thing to do.

Our John is a diligent manager and does his job well. He prepared a list of more than 150 advertising channels, came up with his own medium for each channel with correctly selected text and graphics, made fine-tuning audience settings, marked all ads with utm-tags and launched all advertising campaigns.

A month later, he received statistics from advertising channels and began creating a report. He carefully brought together the entire audience for each advertising channel and medium and synchronized it with the business's CRM using utm-tags having received data on the channels that brought the most sales. Next, he selected the best channels that provided the greatest influx of profit, and went to the owner to ask for a larger budget for the next month.

I think this picture is generally understandable and familiar. But why have I decided to mention it? What did John do wrong? And what in a way does the owner who came up with this way of evaluating his work do wrong? In order to understand this, we will return to the process of preparing advertising campaigns and see that in one of the moments John made a small mistake. He indicated the address of the website where the users should go after clicking on the advertising medium incorrectly.

Now, let's imagine that everything else that the manager did for this advertising campaign — the choice of channel, medium, audience settings, display time, and so on — turned out to be super accurate and hit the target audience, but none of it reached the site and were unable to buy the product being sold. That is, the report for this campaign contains zeros, and the management decides to abandon the channel in favor of others. But it turns out that they abandoned an excellent channel of communication with customers and lost sales.

In order to avoid such problems, it is necessary to separate two processes from each other: the first is attracting potential clients and the second is converting potential clients into real ones. That is why such a division is made in the diagram: potential clients are on one side of the box, and real clients are on the other. In the following chapters, we will return to this issue and consider the importance of this division using an example.

Now, let's see what this framework looks like from a unit economics perspective, how it helps us get the gross and contribution margin numbers, and what we can do with this knowledge in future in order to benefit the product we are developing.

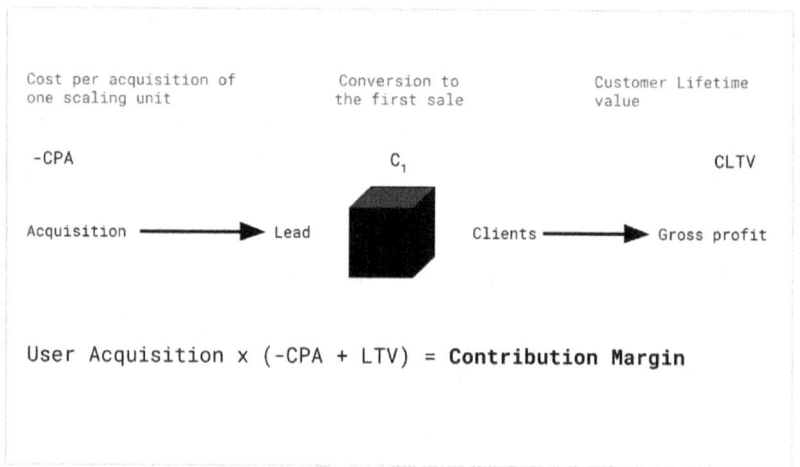

User Acquisition x (-CPA + LTV) = **Contribution Margin**

So, if the marketing specialist's efforts are aimed at attracting or, correctly speaking, scaling potential clients, the contribution margin is the product of the contribution margin per potential client by the number of these potential clients.

User Acquisition is the number of attracted users, or, as I will further on call them, scaling units. And this, actually, is what the work of the responsible for attracting the audience in the company should result in.

CPA is the cost per acquisition of one recruited scaling unit, and LTV is the gross profit per a lead. In this passage, it is explained why I use CLTV referring to the client's gross profit in the sense that David Skok intended it. It is important for me to separate these two gross profits from each other.

To understand what a gross profit per scaling unit is, let's look at an example. If one hundred potential clients give one real one, then the conversion is 1%. If this one real client brings 1000 rubles in gross profit, then this thousand must be divided among all potential clients. Then, it turns out that there are ten rubles of gross profit per a potential client.

At the same time, if we look at the figure, we will see that the parameters that are usually known are indicated at the top We know how much we spend on scaling, we know what percentage of leads become actual customers, which means we know C_1 conversion, and finally, we know what gross profit the business receives from its customers.

We see that conversion seems to separate two worlds: the world of potential clients (leads) and the world of real clients. At the same time, it connects the essences of both worlds: for example,

$$LTV = CLTV \times C_1.$$

Thus, we obtain the final formula for calculating the contribution margin on the flow of scaling units.

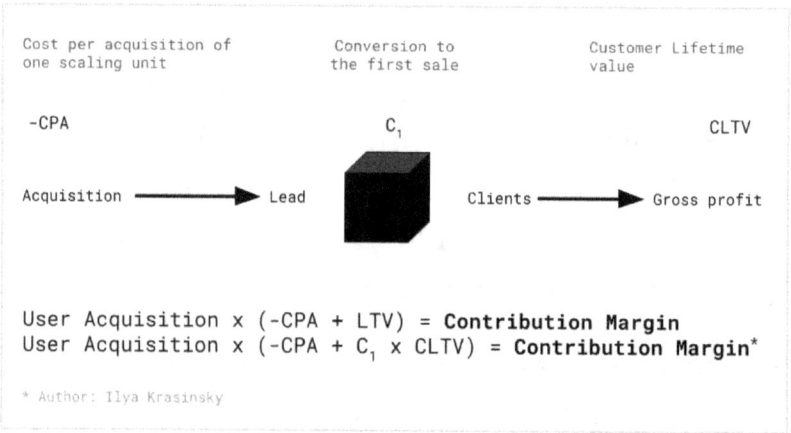

Cost per acquisition of one scaling unit

Conversion to the first sale

Customer Lifetime value

$-CPA$ C_1 $CLTV$

Acquisition ──────▶ Lead   Clients ──────▶ Gross profit

```
User Acquisition x (-CPA + LTV) = Contribution Margin
User Acquisition x (-CPA + C₁ x CLTV) = Contribution Margin*
```

* Author: Ilya Krasinsky

Ilya Krasinsky derived this formula when he was trying to develop a way to manage the creation and launch of a product using unit economics. All you have to do now is to figure out how to calculate gross profit.

```
C₁   = (Buyers / UA)
CLTV = (AOV - COGS) x APC - 1sCOGS
LTV  = CLTV x C₁

AOV     - average order value
COGS    - cost of good sold
1sCOGS  - first sale COGS
APC     - average payment count
```

So, the first defines the essence of conversion. In mathematical terms, this is a coefficient that varies from 0 to 1 or from 0 to 100%. At the same time, in unit economics, it binds together entities from the same set, namely, the set of potential clients, because only representatives of this set can become real clients. In other words, we cannot have more real clients than there were potential ones.

It's important to pay attention to how conversion is calculated in your business. If you use solutions for collecting analytics in a CRM system or on a website (such as Google Analytics), you must definitely read the instructions and see what the creators of these solutions meant by conversion. Make sure you know how it is calculated and whether it is possible to configure the service in such a way that it will consider the data needed in unit economics. Otherwise, you will get incorrect values. In the following chapters, it is demonstrated how disastrous it can be for a business.

Now, let's look at the CLTV formula. It is clearly visible that this is still the same gross profit, but it is multiplied by APC (Average Payment Count) — the average number of payments per client. And a certain 1sCOGS is subtracted — these are additional (indeed, additional!) costs that we incur on the very first sale. Other than that, this is our usual gross profit, the difference between the average check (AOV, Average Order Value) and the COGS prime cost of the transaction.

1sCOGS requires a separate attention. This is a very insidious value: startups often do not take it into account which can lead to bankruptcy. A great example of such a value is various commissioning works, supply of equipment to the client in order to begin work, and so on. If you do it for free or don't take it into account in the economics, it can lead to dire consequences.

It is important to understand that this APC reminds us that we consider the whole economics of the client during the whole time of his interaction with our company.

Now, if we combine the gross and contribution margin formulas, we will see that in order to calculate contribution margin, we need to take only seven variables into account (only six if we don't count 1sCOGS).

UA	C_1	AOV	COGS	APC	CPA	CM
1000	0.10%	1300.00	900.00	1.43	15.00	-14 428.00

⬇

UA	C_1	AOV	COGS	APC	CPA	CM
150 000	0.43%	1500.00	800.00	6.18	12.00	1 000 000.00

The top line shows the current economics (we are not yet considering the situation with a product that has not yet been launched; this will be discussed separately).

In general, at the moment, we have some values of the product metrics. And we know what our contribution margin is. At the same time, we remember that we need it in order to cover fixed costs and ensure a set level of profit. If this condition is not met (in our example, the value is generally negative - this means that we spend more on attracting customers than we earn from them), then we need to find a configuration of metrics that will allow us to achieve the required amount of contribution margin. For example, fixed costs are 750,000 rubles, and we want to make a profit of 250,000 rubles. This means that the contribution margin should be 1,000,000 rubles. All we need to do is to find out what values of the metrics will allow us to reach this million.

This may seem difficult to calculate. However, the main problem is that there is an infinite number of values of these metrics at which we obtain the required amount of contribution margin.

And from this infinite variety of options, we need to choose those that are achievable in reality.

There are three main restrictions. The first restriction is the market: the value of this metrics is limited by the size of the market. Imagine that you can reach the required contribution margin only if you have 10,000,000,000 potential customers. But the whole population of the Earth wouldn't be enough to get this amount of people, which means it is impossible to get so many potential clients, and your business will not reach the given level of contribution margin this way. The second restriction is competence: for example, you need to change the conversion from

0.1% to 2.3%, but your team does not have the appropriate knowledge and experience. Thus, you will not be able to influence the metrics. And the final third restriction is mathematical: some metrics change within strictly fixed limits. For example, conversion can be from 0 to 100%, COGS cannot be less than zero, and so on.

Unit economics for mixed models

In 2014, Vlad's car broke down and the engine died. Vlad lived in Novosibirsk and owned a Japanese car with right-hand drive. The car was not officially imported to Russia, and it was not possible to repair it. Then he decided to try to find the engine at an auto wrecker. To do this, it was necessary to take a directory of enterprises in the region. Luckily, it was within reach — 2GIS, a new service offering digital maps and city guides, had just been developed and launched in Novosibirsk. So, Vlad began calling all the auto wreckers. But no one could immediately give him an answer whether such an engine was available or not, what the price was, and so on. Then the owner of the car expanded his search: now he was interested in auto wreckers within a radius of

250 km from Novosibirsk. The distance was chosen due to the necessity to arrive, to pick up the engine and to return back the same day.

After having searched for quite some time, he noticed that this industry was not at all automated and needed improvement. Vlad came up with a business: he went to the managers of auto wreckers and offered them to use his software and conduct an inventory in order to enter all their goods into a single database. It was agreed.

Then he figured out how to collect a huge number of search queries of people looking for the same products. Generally speaking, it was easy for him, as he had just faced the same problem and understood exactly what he was looking for and how. The idea behind his business was that people search for car parts online because they are used to searching for such products on the Internet. This is not a product for regular merchandise. We do not know where to buy such goods, and when we are faced with the necessity to purchase them, we reflexively go online.

Auto wreckers do not know how to attract traffic from the search systems to their web-pages, if they even have websites, and getting a full-fledged order in such a way is an impossible task for them. At the same time, everything in the sphere of automobiles is quite expensive for search advertising, and you have to pay a lot of money for a small number of orders. In general, the owners of such companies were dissatisfied with the Internet.

Vlad knew how to customize the advertising much better than the car wreckers and he developed the solution that made it possible to receive cheap search traffic and redirect customer requests to those companies that had the necessary auto parts. When a user went from a search engine to Vlad's website, he immediately saw exactly what he was looking for and understood approximately where this product was available and at what price. All they had to do was simply leave their phone numbers. Customers were told that they would receive quotes for their order within 20 minutes. At this point, the request was forwarded to the computers of the relevant company, and the company was asked to make a choice, agree to become a supplier and make an offer to the client, or refuse it. If the company refused to work with the client, then nothing happened. But if it agreed, then a small amount of money was debited from the company's account for the transferred phone number. In addition, if the auto wrecker did not make a choice within several minutes, then it was considered that the company refused the client, but the money was still debited. In this way, Vlad taught auto wreckers to respond to user requests and do it much faster than within the stated 20 minutes.

What benefits did auto wreckers receive? Vlad knew how to attract search traffic well and, most importantly, how to do it for a lower price. He sold it to final suppliers of goods and ensured a high conversion turned into orders that ultimately led to a decrease in the cost of a client for the auto wrecker. And that, of course, was beneficial to the auto wreckers themselves. The programmer has created an excellent system that brought the win-win principle[11] in effect. Now, let's try to calculate the economics of such a product and evaluate the profitability of Vlad's business.

Up to this point, we have only considered the classical, or as I call it, the basic unit economics model, in which a product is created for a customer who uses it and pays for it. This model was actually brought to its current form by Ilya Krasinsky, who at that time was working with startups in a venture fund and was helping new companies with their business models.

However, products like Vlad's, or, for example, mass media operating at the expense of selling the advertising and some other business models cannot be calculated using the approach described above.

The key problem in describing unit economics for this type of business is that in order to understand how satisfied the customer is we need product metrics. The values of the metrics

---

[11] Win-win is an approach that is based on the idea of the possibility of such interaction between the parties (in negotiations, conflict, etc.), in which both parties benefit

here are calculated through the assessment of such economic indicators as an average check (AOV), costs (COGS), frequency of purchases (APC), etc. In this case, the consumers do not show such indicators.

At the end of 2014, I happened to meet Vlad and was involved in the task of building a unit economics model for his business. About six months later, I was working on exactly the same task for another startup that was engaged in attracting clients to fitness centers. During this work, I formulated an approach to describing the unit economics for mixed monetization models, as I called them.

A mixed model is a business containing not two parties, a buyer and a seller as in the usual model, but three — a buyer, a seller and the business itself. In this case, the business produces a product that is used by the buyers and the sellers at the same time. In Vlad's case, he played the role of a business with a product used by the buyers (people looking for spare parts) and the sellers (auto wreckers). In the case of the mass media, the publication itself produces the content, the readers consume it and the advertisers pay the media business for the readers reached. Another interesting case is c2c (customer to customer) models. For example, classifieds, in which there is a business (the owner of the classifieds) and there are users of the service, who can be both sellers and buyers at the same time. Moreover, initially the service does not know what role the user will perform at the time of using it.

To describe the unit economics of such a product, you need to understand how the money moves within such a business and what efforts are expended to ensure that all participants are satisfied. The key problem is that if in the basic model the main consumer of the product was the one who pays for it, then in mixed models the paying party may often not use the product at all (for example, in mass media advertising models), or use a completely different product (as in the case with Vlad's business).

To create this model, I used a little trick that I learned when I was still working in science and doing research. The approach was to place all available information on one surface so as to fill in the known quantities. And then, looking at the resulting picture, try to see what can be done with it.

Since our models have two sides, I decided to describe the unit economics for each side separately. To do this, I simply wrote a standard table with metrics and entered the values that I knew into the cells. Let's look at the example of Vlad's business.

	UAlead	Clead	L	SP	NS	APClead			CPAlead	IR
leads										
	UA	C1	B	AOV	COGS	APC	CLTV	LTV	CPA	CM
customers										

I wrote down everything I knew about his business in a table: "lead" refers to the customers who are looking for spare parts, and "customer" refers to auto wreckers. We knew how many buyers are attracted per month from search queries and how many of them leave their phone numbers, which means we had an understanding of conversion.

It was also known that one phone number was sold for 25 rubles and, on average, each number was forwarded to 2.5 car wreckers. To display this data, I created the Sale Price (SP) and Number of Sales (NS) metrics. It turned out that Vlad's service began to be used by car repair specialists, and the average number of transactions per customer was APC = 1.1.

Regarding auto wreckers, we knew the number of companies that were about to connect to the service as the negotiations with them were underway, as well as the conversion rate they were connecting with. In addition, it was known that one auto wrecker, having connected to the service, does not disconnect from it for about 10 months (in fact, more, but at the time of development of the model there was no other data, all connected auto wreckers worked with Vlad). The price of communication with one auto wrecker was also known – CPA.

All this ultimately gave this picture:

	UAlead	Clead	L	BP	NS	APClead			CPAlead	IR
leads	10,000	25.00%	2,500	25.00	2.50	1.10			2.65	80.00%
	UA	C1	B	AOV	COGS	APC	CLTV	LTV	CPA	CM
customers	40	10.00%	4			10.00			3,000.00	

The top line is associated with buyers of spare parts and does not bring us any money. However, the quantity of transactions completed and the general satisfaction of the buyers depend on the quality of a product we make for them, which is evaluated by the quickness of response of auto wreckers to requests, quality of the goods, etc. Vlad made a product both for auto wreckers and the buyers.

On the other hand, auto wreckers were the ones who actually paid Vlad for each phone number provided. And to calculate the contribution margin from them, it was necessary to calculate the average check and costs. What do these quantities depend on? First of all, they depend on the number of leads (potential buyers), the information about whom is bought by auto wreckers. As it turned out, not all phone numbers received by Vlad were sold. A certain number did not find a response: either there was no spare part, or for some reason no one wanted to get in touch. One way or another, about 20% of the information was not in demand. To capture this parameter, I introduced the IR (Inventory Release) metrics.

Thus, the money from the sale of all phone numbers that found a response from auto wreckers can be calculated using the formula $NS \times SP \times APC_{LEAD} \times L \times IR$. If this number is divided by the number of clients, then we get the value of the average check that an auto wrecker pays for the acquisition of phone numbers.

$$AOV = NS \times SP \times APC_{LEAD} \times L \times IR / B$$

We proceed similarly with the calculation of COGS. Technically, Vlad only incurred expenses in order to attract customers to his service and get their phone numbers. For this, he launched a complex advertising campaign. In fact, this was the hardest thing Vlad was keen at doing, his magic — he knew how to attract a huge number of buyers to auto wreckers at the lowest prices on the market. He spent only 2.65 rubles per transition of a lead from search engines to his product. His total costs of purchasing leads were $UA_{LEAD} \times CPA_{LEAD}$. And all these costs were evenly distributed among the auto wreckers in their part of the unit economics.

$$COGS = UA_{LEAD} \times CPA_{LEAD} / B$$

Please, note that we are not taking into account the share of the acquisition of phone numbers by auto wreckers here, because, regardless of whether Vlad sold the number or not, he incurred the costs of purchasing it.

Now, you have everything you need to calculate the contribution margin using Krasinski's formula.

	UAlead	Clead	L	SP	NS	APClead			CPAlead	IR
leads	10,000	25.00%	2,500	25.00	2.50	1.10			2.65	80.00%
	UA	C1	B	AOV	COGS	APC	CLTV	LTV	CPA	CM
customers	40	10.00%	4	34,375.00	6,825.00	10.00	277,500.00	27,750.00	3,000.00	990,000.00

Pivot, or How unit economics helps a business grow

In fact, it often happens that you cannot find the configuration of metrics you need. This is generally normal. What should be done in this case? It is necessary to look for a new business model. A good example is Uber.

UberCab　Key Differentiators

- **Members Only** - Respectable clientele
- **1-click hailing** – "Pickup here in 5 mins"
- **Fast Response time** – easier than calling
- **Luxury automobiles** – Mercedes Sedans
- **Great drivers** – "Rate your trip" feature
- **High-tech solution:** Geo-aware auto-dispatch
- **Optimized fleet** – Logistical LBS software

In 2008, Uber presented itself as a premium ride-hailing company focusing on the San Francisco market and later expanding to Manhattan and New York. The company wanted to change the premium ride-hailing market and estimated its capacity at $4.2 billion, planning to reach an annual turnover of $1 billion.

UberCab

Potential Outcomes

- Best-Case Scenario
  - Becomes market leader, $1B+ in yearly revenue
- Realistic Success Scenario
  - Gets 5% of the top 5 US Cities
  - Generates 20-30M+ per year profit
- Worst-Case Scenario
  - Remains a 10 car, 100 client service in SF
  - Time-saver for San-Francisco based executives

20

Later, it turned out that even if the company manages to capture the entire market for all transportation services in San Francisco, it still will not reach the set level of profit. In fact, while solving the problem of finding the optimal configuration of unit economics metrics for their business model, they were unable to find the required product metrics that would allow them to obtain a sufficient level of contribution margin to cover their fixed costs and bring the company to a given level of profit.

The company had to look for new ways to develop the business, determine how to change the model so that its metrics would allow Uber to reach the desired level of contribution margin.

As a result, the company came to the idea that it was necessary to occupy the entire transportation market, since, unlike premium ride-hailing services in wealthy US cities, the private cab market, or simply taxis, operated all over the world. The key idea was the ability to call a taxi from the application from any place in the world and get a fairly cheap ride. This idea was applicable to any audience, and not just to the demanding audience of wealthy US cities.

The demonstrated flexibility allowed the company to significantly increase market coverage, that is, the number of permissible scaling units, and obtain the required level of contribution margin even taking the decrease in the average check into account. For startups, such changes are usually called Pivot, or business model reversal.

Scaling a business

Search for growth points

Three women, who had achieved success by the age of thirty, worked in senior positions in corporations maintaining a very high standard of living. One of them had a child. It is known that having children is a big responsibility and the child requires care 24/7. Mothers are tired, they want to lead a normal life and at the same time raise their children in such a way that they stay happy, healthy and smart.

We usually call this a problem, but the women considered it as an opportunity to build a business.

They left their jobs and used their savings to hire a methodologist who prepared various educational and developmental materials for them. It was selected according to the child's gender, age and interests. You can see one of such sets on the slide. They launched a startup — "Two Palms".

The idea was as follows. They planned to create a website for the mothers similar to our heroines - living in big cities, with high incomes, having children and wanting to raise them healthy, smart and happy. Having visited the website, such mothers could choose a kit, pay for it and get two hours of free time.

When I gave this example at my presentations, I often asked a question: "Imagine that you are an investor to whom such a project was presented, and you need to make a decision whether to invest in it or not. What decision will you make? Based on their answers, the listeners formed four groups. The first ones did not want to invest because they did not like the idea: they believed that the child would not play, that the mothers would not get free time in such a way. Some of them added that their child definitely wouldn't play with that. The second group, on the contrary, was immediately ready to invest because they saw a huge potential, a large market and prospects. The third group asked questions: what is the market like? How much money is required? The fourth group kept silent — such people are present among any audience.

In fact, both those who were in favor of the project and those who were against it turned out to be wrong, since all their decisions were based on personal experience and not on the information about the project.

The main conclusion we can make from this example is that we do make decisions in personal life and in business in such a way, but it is not the right way to decide. And we shouldn't make any decisions based on a story alone.

When I ask the audience what can help them make a decision, they usually require to see the figures that the startup relies on. Namely, the cost of the box, the size of the market, etc. Let's see what this startup demonstrated.

```
Monthly subscription
Box price                            1400
Direct cost                           600
Delivery and packing                  300
Marketing (extimate)                  300
Profit                                200


This year data shows that each client bought two
boxes on average
```

This is the second slide from the "Two Palms" presentation. They sold the box for 1,400 rubles. The contents cost 600 rubles, the cost of production and delivery to the client was 300 rubles, the cost of attracting a client was estimated at another 300 rubles. We can see that the team has calculated the profit. In addition, they applied for the investment a year after the launch, and statistics show that during this time, each client bought two boxes on average. The team was looking for money to expand the sales market and scale the business.

If we demonstrate this slide and ask the audience whether there are those who changed their decision regarding the investment in the project, then we will see different opinions again: some will say that the profit is too small, some will not like the cost, etc. But in fact, this data is not enough to make an investment decision. Let's look at the last slide from the presentation of our heroines.

```
Before acceleration program      After acceleration program
• 650 box sold for 12 months     • 650 box sold for 3 months
  (50 per month)                    (200 per month)
• Accumulated earning - 850k     • Earnings for 3 months - 850k
• 300 clients                    • +400 new clients
• 300 emails                     • +1000 new email
• 10 000 user on site            • 15 000 users on site
• Self-financing                 • +$150 000 from business
                                   angels
```

What do we see on this slide? Firstly, the team attracted investments; secondly, investments were received under the acceleration program during which the business grew fourfold.

If I were to ask now who is ready to invest in this project, the picture would not probably change much: some would be "for" the investment, some would stay "against" it. But to answer this question, you just need to calculate the unit economics and see how well it converges. That is, whether the contribution margin of a given project is positive or not.

```
CAC = 300
CLTV = (1400 - 900) x 2 = 1000
```

The cost of attracting a client is 300 rubles, and the gross profit is calculated as the average check (1,400 rubles) minus the cost of the contents of the box (600 rubles), as well as the box itself and its delivery to the client (300 rubles). It turns out that by selling one box the company receives 500 rubles in gross profit. But each client buys two boxes on average, which means the gross profit per client is 1000 rubles.

```
CAC = 300
CLTV = (1400 - 900) x 2 = 1000

ROMI = (1000 - 300) / 300 > 230%!
```

Thus, by investing 300 rubles in attracting a client, the company receives back 1000 rubles in gross profit, or more than 230% return on marketing investments.

Looking at such numbers, you usually want to scale your business. But the startups understand the meaning of this phrase differently. What does "to scale" mean? What exactly will we increase? If we collect the answers and analyze them, we will see that the majority believes that it is necessary to increase the number of clients. That is, we will scale clients.

> *The number of customers (B) is not a decision-making indicator, as it depends on conversion (C) and the number of users (UA).*

However, as we remember, in the process of scaling we increase the number of potential clients, and this example once again confirms this fact.

The number of customers depends on several metrics: namely, the number of potential clients who were attracted to the website, and the conversion of these potential clients into real ones. How will the number of clients increase?

Moreover, these two processes must be developed by different people and will require different costs, as the improvement of these processes requires two completely different solutions. This means that we cannot say for sure how exactly the number of clients should be increased.

That is why, when scaling, you need to clearly separate potential customers from real ones. To do this, we need conversion data. It is given in the presentation:

```
CAC = 300
CLTV = (1400 - 900) x 2 = 1000

C   = 4.33%
CPA = CAC x C = 13
LTV = CLTV x C = 43.3
```

The team reported a conversion rate of 4.33%, which means we can calculate the cost of acquiring each lead and the gross profit attributable to it. It is important to note that in real life such calculations are not being made: to determine the cost of acquiring a potential client, one must simply divide the marketing costs by the number of potential clients.

However, such an entry demonstrates once again that conversion connects two worlds — the world of potential customers (CPA and LTV) and the real ones (CAC and CLTV).

```
UA      = 15 000
C       = 4.33%
CPA     = 13
CLTV    = 1000 / LTV = 43.3

ROMI > 230%, each website visitor brings 30.
What do we do next?
```

While nothing was changed, we know that the team has attracted 15,000 people, the conversion rate was 4.33%, the cost of attracting one potential client was 13 rubles, and the gross profit per potential client was 43.3 rubles. Thus, each visitor by the very fact of entering the website brought 30 rubles in contribution margin.

Now, it's much easier to answer the question of what to do next. Obviously, increasing conversion is a very complex process, while the process of attracting the audience is more understandable. And if the market is large enough, you can even calculate how many potential customers you need to attract in order to get the required contribution margin.

Before we continue our research into the "Two Palms" business, we need to stop and look at the conclusions we have drawn. In fact, we see a growing business, and right now its main principle of growth is scaling the number of potential customers. To do this, the startup applies for investments. And if we do not take some issues that we will discuss further into account, investments are usually provided.

However, I want to draw your attention to the figures provided by the "Two Palms". On this slide, I highlighted two numbers that, in my opinion, cause mistrust. The main question is why did I choose these exact two figures? What is wrong with them?

```
UA      = 15 000
C       = 4.33%
CPA     = 13
CLTV    = 1000 / LTV = 43.3
The number of purchases made by one client - 2
```

First, let's look at the conversion. To understand what is wrong with it, we must first remember what we are doing when analyzing any indicator or metric. When we talk about a particular metric, we usually mean comparison. It is not yet clear what to compare conversion with, although even a simple comparison with the market and competitors will do. But let's start with what conversion can be like.

Let me remind you that conversion is a coefficient that shows what proportion of potential customers turns into the real ones. The conversion can range from 0 to 1 or from 0 to 100%. Knowing this, how to estimate the conversion rate of 4.33%? On the one hand, we see that it is closer to zero than to 100%, which means it is not so high. On the other hand, we know that the average conversion rate in e-commerce is close to 1%. Therefore, the conversion of 4.33% is actually high.

Leaving aside the fact that this conversion rate is suspiciously higher than the market average, how else can this indicator be characterized? All buyers coming for any product are divided into two large groups: those who came to make the first purchase, and those who came for the second and subsequent purchases. And the behavior of these groups varies greatly. In fact, they come for different goods.

The former come to buy the trust. Indeed, the trust: they believe that they will buy a solution to their problem, but in fact the purchase might not solve the problem and might even turn out to be not what it seemed and create new problems. Therefore, the former ones buy the trust.

The latter simply want to pay money and receive a product or a service as quickly and simply as possible. They don't want to remember their passwords in your store, don't want to log in, etc. — they just want to buy a product.

Note that these two audiences behave very differently. When making a purchasing decision, they are guided by different considerations. But at the same time, the interaction of companies with them (for example, through websites) looks exactly the same to both of these audiences. This is why the online conversion is so low in absolute terms.

But let's get back to the company we are analyzing. The team made a mistake calculating the conversion. Further on, I'll show you how exactly it happened. For now, let's pay attention to the fact that when calculating conversions, you cannot mix purchases from these two audiences. The fact is that in unit economics, the conversion that separates the potential buyers from the real ones is precisely the conversion of the first purchase. That is why it is marked with the index $1 - C_1$.

The actual conversion to the first purchase $C_1 = 1.57\%$!
In average, one client was buying **1.4** boxes, not 2!

The actual conversion turned out to be 1.57%, and the average number of transactions was 1.4, not two. We will discuss this specifically further in the book.

Now, let's see what these mistakes led to.

```
The actual conversion to the first purchase
C₁ = 1.57%!
In average, one client was buying 1.4 boxes,
not 2!

So
CLTV = (1400 - 900) x 1.4 = 700
```

According to the original calculations, the gross profit per client was 1,000 rubles; on average, a client made two purchases. Now, we see that in fact the client made an average of 1.4 purchases (that is, 30% less), and the gross profit was 700 rubles (which is also 30% less). Fundamentally, it would seem that nothing has changed here.

```
The actual conversion to the first purchase
C₁ = 1.57%!
In average, one client was buying 1.4 boxes,
not 2!

So
CLTV = (1400 - 900) x 1.4 = 700
LTV = 700 x 1.57% = 10.99!
```

But the gross profit per potential client has changed catastrophically: according to the original calculations it was 43.3 rubles, and now it has fallen to 10.99 rubles. That is, it turned out to be four times less.

```
The actual conversion to the first purchase
C₁ = 1.57%!
In average, one client was buying 1.4 boxes,
not 2!

So
CLTV = (1400 - 900) x 1.4 = 700
LTV = 700 x 1.57% = 10.99!
ROMI = (10.99 - 13) / 13 = -15%!
Economics not converge!
```

And the economics turned from positive that begged for business expansion, to negative. If you scale such economics, only losses will scale. This means that we should think not about scaling, but about how to bring the economics together.

However, it is too early to draw final conclusions, "Two Palms" can still show us how important data is for decision-making in business. The point is, if your conversion doesn't add up, it is still not a problem. Moreover, many investors are interested in businesses whose economics does not add up — not just any business, of course, but the one whose economics can be improved. This allows the investor to enter a business that has the potential to grow. Due to diverging economics, it will have a lower valuation, which means it will bring more benefits to the investor if it is successful.

Therefore, it is important to understand whether the economics can be improved. Let's start with the conversion. We already know that the average conversion in e-commerce is about 1% and the conversion of the company in question is more than 1.5%, which is higher than the market indicators. However, we should be concerned that this is still a very small conversion in absolute terms. That is, more than 98% of potential customers do not buy anything. What's wrong? Let's figure it out.

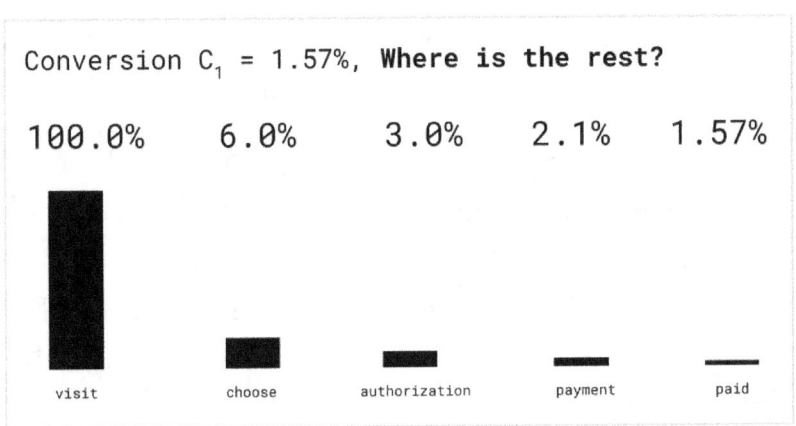

Conversion C_1 = 1.57%, **Where is the rest?**

100.0%	6.0%	3.0%	2.1%	1.57%
visit	choose	authorization	payment	paid

This is what the sales funnel on the company website looks like. All conversions are shown in relation to the first step. At the input — 100% of potential clients who came to the site. And the result is 1.57% conversion. These are the clients who bought something.

Entering the website, a person must make a choice. Namely, he is asked to indicate the child's gender, age and interests. These three steps are required and it is impossible to buy the product without going through this stage. And, as we see, only 6% of the audience copes with it.

Next, the potential buyer must provide information about himself, his contact details, delivery address, etc. Of all those who saw this window (and this, as we remember, is 6%), only half — 3% — managed to fill it out.

The next step is entering payment card information, and only 70% of those who reach this stage (or 2.1% of the audience from the beginning of the funnel) fill this field out. In the end, only 1.57% of the entire funnel completes the payment.

What can we learn analyzing this data? First of all, it is desirable to understand at what stage does the company lose the biggest amount of money that is the easiest to get back? At first glance, the question seems simple. However, some people will say that it is the first step, because the losses are the greatest there – 94%. Others will note that it's the last one, because they heard somewhere that you need to optimize the funnel from the end: after all, that's where the hottest users are, who overcame all the obstacles and abandoned the purchase at the last step.

The correct answer for any entrepreneur and product developer to remember is: "I don't know." When operating in conditions of uncertainty, you must be honest with yourself. To answer the question asked above, you need to know what competencies the team has that will allow you to adjust certain steps and thereby influence the funnel. Has everything possible already been done or is there more that can be done? Since we do not have an answer to these questions, we cannot answer the main question.

It is true that it is recommended to look for the growth point in the funnel from the end, and I will explain later why it is so. As for the first step, not everything is simple here either: losing 94% of the audience is very bad. Essentially, this means that people do not trust the company. We remember that those who come to buy for the first time (and when we talk about conversion, we mean them) come for the trust. And instead of being informed about the essence of the proposed value (we remember from the presentation that this is two hours of personal life) potential clients are forced to indicate the gender, age and other information about the child. Of course, people don't believe that the product offered will solve their problem, and they simply leave. This means that the team has not learned how to activate potential clients and lead them to a deal. That is, it does not control conversion.

Now let's look at another metric — the cost of attracting one potential client (CPA). The company indicated that it is 13 rubles, which is quite low for the niche in which they worked.

Having analyzed the team's marketing skills, they immediately realized the obvious: they did not know how to advertise themselves. So, they hired an agency that was responsible for the number of visitors and the price. And in general, everyone was happy until the company conducted analysis of the audience by the acquisition channels. It turned out that only six clients came through the paid channels in January, and the rest came through free, viral channels.

```
CPA = 13!
In January, 118 out of 124 clients
who made a purchase came from
Direct type in, Google Search, etc.
```

This means that the audience initially knew what they were looking for, and the main consequence of this is that scaling for money will not work. This means that the team cannot manage marketing either. It turns out that there is nothing to scale here; we need to start with adding up the economics.

Goldratt's Theory of Constraints

To study the issues of scaling a business and using unit economics for this further, as well as further research into the "Two Palms" business, we will need to get acquainted with Goldratt's Theory of Constraints since this tool is vital for further work. This theory was developed by Eliyahu Goldratt in the late 70s and early 80s of the XX century, and it was developed to optimize industrial production. Here we need to make a short digression to explain why we needed it and how it relates to unit economics.

On the tenth day of the month of Tishrei, devout Jews completed a ten-day period of repentance spending most of their time in prayer and attending the synagogue. Yom Kippur is one of the most revered and important holidays, a celebration of atonement and reconciliation. It is so important that even secular Israelis observe it. At this time, the streets are empty, transport systems, including airports, do not work. People celebrate an important day for them.

On this day, on October 6, 1973, at 2 p.m., the military might of two powers, Egypt and Syria, fell upon Israel at once. Both of these states could not forgive Israel for the military losses they suffered as a result of the six-day war and, having developed a joint plan for revenge, struck on the most peaceful holiday of the country.

Initially, as a result of an unexpected attack from two sides at once, the armies of Egypt and Syria were victorious, but after 18 days the war ended when the Israeli army was only 101 km from Cairo and 40 km from Damascus. All participants in the battles suffered significant losses, but it all ended in the victory of Israel. Although, in Arab countries victory is given to Egypt and Syria for propaganda purposes.

In general, this was not the first and not the last war between Israel and its Arab neighbors, but it affected not only the parties involved, but also the whole world. The world has changed beyond recognition, and now we live by the rules that differ significantly from the rules adopted before the Yom Kippur War.

After the end of the war, a strong political crisis erupted in Israel; the people were dissatisfied that the country was not ready for such tests. As a result, Israeli Prime Minister Golda Meyer and the entire cabinet of her government resigned, and high-ranking military personnel responsible for army training, as well as for intelligence, in particular in the Egyptian direction, were removed from their positions.

Arab countries suffered huge losses and lost part of their territory. In general, we can talk about the defeat of the armies of Egypt and Syria, but the successes in the first days of the war were, though a small, but consolation for them.

The main result of the Yom Kippur War was the revenge of the Arab countries on Israel's allies, namely the United States and Western European countries. The oil cartel states that include mainly Arab and African countries that supported Egypt and Syria in the war have imposed an oil embargo on the United States and its allies, Great Britain, Canada, the Netherlands and Japan.

It's hard to imagine now, but the Arab states that according to the official economic theory belong to the "third world" have imposed sanctions against the United States and its allies. In addition, OAPEC raised oil prices for the whole world from 3 to 12 dollars per barrel.

This led to a severe oil crisis. The graph shows the price of oil in US dollars per barrel from 1861 to 2015, showing the price in nominal dollars at the time of sale and in 2015 US dollars.

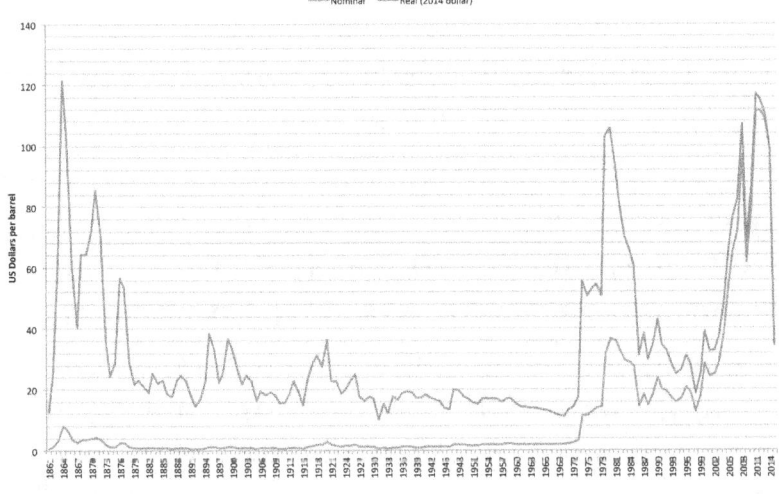

CRUDE OIL PRICES SINCE 1861

You can clearly see that the price of oil changed dramatically in the 1970s. This led to major changes in the world. And these changes happened despite the fact that the embargo lasted only about six months. Let's look at what the crisis caused by the Yom Kippur War led to.

Let's start, probably, with the USSR: since the Arab countries imposed an embargo, the Soviet Union became one of the largest oil suppliers for Western countries in the world market. This ultimately led to a significant flow of oil dollars.

[12] https://en.wikipedia.org/wiki/1973_oil_crisis

The inflow of foreign currency allowed the USSR to survive for another 10 years, the money was used to support the economy and finance military projects, such as the war in Afghanistan. However, the graph clearly shows that by the mid-80s the oil price had rolled back from its peak values and this ultimately led to the collapse of the Soviet economy. The Soviets were forced to launch perestroika, develop market relations and in 1991, having broken up into independent states, the great empire ceased to exist. The Cold War ended, the world became unipolar, and for the first time, for all countries, for a while there was basically one ideology left — capitalism. Such were the consequences of a small Arab–Israeli Yom Kippur War for the USSR.

Let's now look at how the embargo affected Western European countries. As a result, of all these developments, for the first time, governments were thinking about how to achieve energy independence. Thus, France and Japan launched powerful programs for the development of nuclear energy. In Europe, energy saving processes were put on a scientific basis, which generally contributed to the development of energy efficiency and now we can see the results of what began with the embargo in 1973 — LED lamps, fuel-efficient engines, the transition to solar and wind energy. Thus, the US allies received an impetus for the development of science and technology. The embargo had the greatest impact on the United States — that was actually what it was intended for. To understand how badly the US suffered, let's look at how dependent the US was on oil in 1973.

The average volume of the eight-cylinder V-shaped engine of the Chevrolet Caprice of those times was 6.5 liters.

And the Chevrolet Impala reached 8 liters! At the same time, Impala consumed 18 liters of gasoline per 100 km on the highway! As a result of the embargo, gasoline in the United States not only sharply increased in price, but also simply disappeared. Some gas stations went bankrupt and began to be used for other purposes, such as houses of worship. The lines at gas stations stretched for kilometers.

The oil crisis affected US business as well, primarily causing serious problems for automakers. The cars of the Big Three (GM,

Ford, Chrysler) were large, expensive and power-hungry. Their sales began to experience a noticeable decline. The consequence of this was the collapse and "bankruptcy" of one of the largest industrial centers in the United States — Detroit. Now, it represents a sad spectacle of its former luxury: loss of population, decline in industry and a significant increase in crime.

Moreover, the competitors decided to take advantage of the situation in the US car market, Toyota becoming one of them.

Taking advantage of the situation, namely the oil crisis and the sharp demand for cars with low fuel consumption, Toyota decided to win American hearts by launching cars with small and gasoline saving engines that American manufacturers did not produce. However, this fact alone was not enough to conquer the US market. The Japanese company faced some questions, the answers to which were necessary for the victory. It was necessary to understand how Americans buy cars, why they buy cars, how they use them, how they choose them, and many other factors.

To find answers, Toyota came up with the following approach: the way to conquer the US market was to create the ideal car for the American family. To understand which car will be in demand, you need to produce a small batch of cars and show it to customers, get feedback from them, make changes to the design of the car and repeat this process until the ideal car is found. In general, this is similar to the actions of modern startupers. Namely — Customer Development.

In order to implement this plan, Toyota had to figure out a way to bypass the economics of the assembly line of a mass product. The fact is that, starting in 1901, at the Randsom Olds plant, cars were assembled on an assembly line. Many believe that conveyor assembly was used at Henry Ford's factories for the first time, but this is not so, as the Oldsmobile plant was the first to use assembly lines, and Ford only improved Olds' solution. Thus, starting with the Curved Dash Oldsmobile, car production follows the simple rule of mass production. The more cars we produce, the lower is the cost per unit.

As we can see, this rule did not allow Toyota to produce small batches in order to find the ideal car. Thus, the Japanese company needed to come up with a way to make the assembly of small batches on an assembly line as cost-effective as possible.

To solve this complex problem, Toyota has come up with many different approaches. Overall, the company managed to implement this idea. In general terms, it all came down to the advent of lean manufacturing. In order to implement this approach, the Japanese had to come up with many interesting things that are now widely used, for example, in programming: tools such as kanban boards, kaizen, etc. This approach is well described in the book "The Toyota Way"[13].

An example of this approach is the release of the second generation of Toyota Sienna minivan. In order to make the perfect car, the head of the development of this minivan, Yuji Yokoya, personally drove more than 85,000 km on the US roads and collected feedback, as well as personal feelings, which ultimately allowed him

---

[13] The Toyota Way: 14 Management Principles from the World's Greatest Manufacturer by Jeffrey Liker

to create the perfect car for the American consumer.

The direction developed by Toyota since the 50s of the 20th century allowed the Japanese company to quickly capture the American market at the time of the crisis caused by the Yom Kippur War. As we can see, in addition to winning a place in the American sun, the company gave the world many useful things, business tools and, of course, one of the best car models.

In the early 1970s, a young physicist, Eliyahu Goldratt, and his brother were recruited to develop a mass production management system for a small poultry farm. The brothers began their work, but were forced to interrupt, since Eliyahu was called to war, the same one with which our story began — the Yom Kippur War. Upon his return, he continued to work on solving business problems. As a result, he and his brother developed a solution that increased the efficiency of the enterprise by 50% without requiring additional resources. However, the company was unable to implement the innovation and spread it to all business processes. As a result, it went bankrupt, and Goldratt returned to the university.

Goldratt formulated his approach to optimizing a production line as the Theory of Constraints. This theory made it possible to quite effectively optimize the production line using simple rules:

- find the narrow space (bottleneck)
- subordinate all the production decisions to a bottleneck
- expand the bottleneck
- find a new bottleneck

In fact, this is an approach similar to the one Toyota used for assembly line optimization. However, Goldratt considered the Japanese company's practices too complex. In addition, he managed to describe his approach in a very simple language that was understandable to everyone. He described his Theory of Constraints in the book "The Goal," which, unlike most boring books on the theory of production management, was published in the format of a business novel. The novel was quite fascinating, but at the same time revealed all the economic processes quite well. In general, Goldratt has written several books, each showing the application of his theory to different types of business ranging from optimizing the assembly line in the production of spare parts — "The Goal", and ending with optimizing warehouse balances in retail — "Isn't It obvious".

If you pay attention to how I write down unit economics metrics (for example, here, in the form of a table), you can see that the columns contain parameters, the cells contain values and the metrics are placed in a certain order.

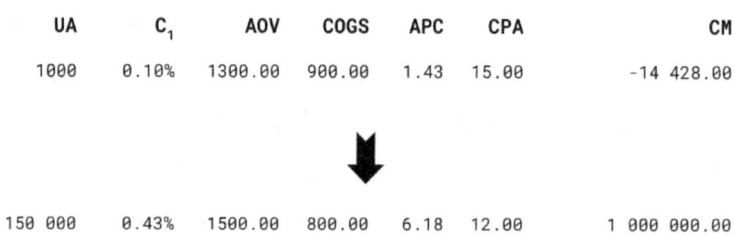

UA	C_1	AOV	COGS	APC	CPA	CM
1000	0.10%	1300.00	900.00	1.43	15.00	-14 428.00
150 000	0.43%	1500.00	800.00	6.18	12.00	1 000 000.00

Such a record can be thought of as a conveyor; at the input we see users who go through various "machines", such as conversion, average check, cost, repeat sales and attraction. And since this is a conveyor, it means that Goldratt's approach — the theory of system constraints — is applicable to it. Now, we can find a bottleneck in our "assembly line", subordinate the company's processes to this bottleneck and expand it. To do this, you just need to see which "machine" of our unit economics, if changed to the minimum value, gives the maximum increase in contribution margin. It is also important to take the resource costs of changing the parameter into account.

In addition, you need to understand that each "machine" is in one way or another connected with business processes in the company, and, therefore, understanding where your bottleneck is, you can focus on solving problems in the right place, rather than being scattered about everything.

For example, if your bottleneck turns out to be C_1 conversion, that is connected to a low activation of the product, then your task is to stop blaming the entire marketing department saying that their advertising is not working, and start figuring out why people come to you for the product and can't get it.

As often happens, we advertise, but managers cannot answer the phone when a client calls us, our employee damages and slowly ships the goods, and the courier steals it. But when the director receives a report on the advertising performance, he sees that the number of sales has not increased, and makes a fundamental decision - the advertisers are to blame for doing their job poorly. Therefore, remember: once you find a bottleneck, subordinate all the company's processes to this place.

Now, we can return to "Two Palms" and figure out how their business could grow. Let's find their bottlenecks.

Focus in business

In previous chapters, we learned that it is too early to scale the "Two Palms" business, since the team must first bring the economy to positive contribution margin values. To do this, we will use Goldratt's Theory of Constraints and learn how to focus in business. After all, you've probably heard this word, but I've almost never come across an explanation of exactly how to do this. So, let me describe it myself.

With the help of unit economics, you can focus on your business, look for growth points, and find the optimal configuration of metrics.

First, let's look at the initial economics of the company and at the same time figure out how the mistake with the conversion was made.

UA	C1	B	AOV	COGS	APC	LTV	LTC	CM
15000	4.33%	650	0.00	0.00	0.00	0.00	0.00	0.00

The number of visitors (15,000) and conversion to the first purchase (4.33%) give us 650, but we remember that the company sold only 650 boxes during the year of operation. That means, the team calculated the conversion incorrectly: it was necessary to divide the number of buyers by the number of visitors, but they divided the number of boxes sold by the number of visitors.

UA	C1	B	AOV	COGS	APC	LTV	LTC	CM
15000	4.33%	650	1,400.00	900.00	2.00	43.30	13.00	454,500.00

As soon as we entered all the data, we saw that the economics in the initial view was positive, which means it required money for scaling. But we know that this economics was counted incorrectly, and two indicators must be corrected.

UA	C1	B	AOV	COGS	APC	LTV	LTC	CM
15000	4.33%	650	1,400.00	900.00	2.00	43.30	13.00	454,500.00
15000	1.57%	236	1,400.00	900.00	2.00	15.70	13.00	40,500.00

We see that a change in conversion from 4.33% to 1.57% (that is, 2.88 times in total) leads to a catastrophic drop in contribution margin: it declines by more than 11 times.

Now, let's change the frequency of transactions: instead of two, we will indicate the real 1.4 transactions per client.

UA	C1	B	AOV	COGS	APC	LTV	LTC	CM
15000	4.33%	650	1,400.00	900.00	2.00	43.30	13.00	454,500.00
15000	1.57%	236	1,400.00	900.00	2.00	15.70	13.00	40,500.00
15000	1.57%	236	1,400.00	900.00	1.40	10.99	13.00	-30,150.00

And now it is clearly visible that in reality the company's economics is negative.

A quick summary of what has been done so far is a simple visualization of how Goldratt's approach applies to production optimization. The essence of this approach is as follows: first, we find a bottleneck — a bottleneck that slows down the entire process; then we subordinate the business to this process, that is, we focus on it and offer solutions that will improve its efficiency. Then, we improve the process moving on to a new bottleneck.

If you look at the table in which the unit economics was calculated, we see that its columns are metrics. At the input we see the number of potential customers (UA) and at the output – the contribution margin (CM). You can think of it as an assembly line, which means you can apply Goldratt's approach to optimizing it. And then the bottleneck in unit economics will be a metric that, when changed by a small amount, gives a multiple increase in contribution margin at the lowest cost of changing the metric.

Actually, in our example it was a conversion.

Let's look at a sample list of tasks that an entrepreneur may face. To decide which tasks need to be done and in what order, we need to determine the tasks, the solution of which would provide the greatest contribution to the contribution margin with the least cost for the solution itself.

```
Task list

1. Reducing the number of steps at the registration stage
2. Push-notifications
3. Creation of onboarding
4. The launch of a new logistics product
5. Funnel optimization
6. CJM analysis
7. Launch of a new promotion
8. Email marketing
9. Situational marketing
0. A solution to increase the number of items in the cart
1. Bags fixing
2. Personal discounts
3. To set up telephony in the customer support department
```

In fact, unit economics makes things easier. First, we find a bottleneck in the model using Goldratt's Theory of Constraints, and then, having determined which metric it is associated with, we generate tasks associated only with that metric. This is the very focus that all startups are advised to think about.

Goldratt's approach will help find the optimal configuration of metrics. At the very beginning, I already talked about how difficult it is to find a configuration that will allow you to reach the desired level of contribution margin. How can we use Goldratt's approach for this?

First, let's look at one more example. Probably, many of you faced such a situation when there are no sales, and the marketer who advertises poorly is to blame for this. Now we will look at a case where there are no sales, but advertising and marketing are not to blame.

UA	C1	B	AOV	COGS	APC	LTV	LTC	CM
15000	1.57%	236	1,400.00	900.00	1.40	10.99	13.00	-30,150.00

If you look closely at the company's indicators, you will see that the contribution margin on the flow of potential clients is determined by the contribution margin of one potential client, namely the difference between LTV and LTC (this is the same as CPA). That is why they are placed next to each other in the table: to make it easier to work with it and immediately see how the economy is shaping up.

In this case, there are two values: 10.99 and 13.00. At the same time, we know that the team did not do marketing, but outsourced everything. But let's assume that it was the company itself, through its own efforts, that achieved effectiveness in advertising and increased the cost of one potential client to 13 rubles. At the same time, we assume that, besides marketing, it can't do anything else.

This only means that employees will be able to put in even more effort and bring this value to 10 rubles. This is quite realistic. Let's see what happens to the economics in this case.

UA	C1	B	AOV	COGS	APC	LTV	LTC	CM
15000	1.57%	236	1,400.00	900.00	1.40	10.99	13.00	-30,150.00
15000	1.57%	236	1,400.00	900.00	1.40	10.99	10.00	14,850.00

As we expected, the economics became positive and can now be scaled up. It will no longer be possible to improve it, since the team, as stated above, can't do anything else. We need to figure out at what value of the metrics the economics will reach a conditional million rubles.

UA	C1	B	AOV	COGS	APC	LTV	LTC	CM
15,000	1.57%	236	1,400.00	900.00	1.40	10.99	13.00	-30,150.00
15,000	1.57%	236	1,400.00	900.00	1.40	10.99	10.00	14,850.00
1,010,101	1.57%	15859	1,400.00	900.00	1.40	10.99	10.00	1,000,000.00

It is clearly seen that with such figures you can reach a million rubles if you attract more than a million potential clients. Even if we put aside the fact that this is a lot in general, the problem is that in the market where the company operates, there are no more than 15,000,000 women of all ages, incomes and interests in total. It means that after 15 months, the team will pass the entire market through its product and reach only 1,000,000 rubles in contribution margin on a monthly cohort.

In other words, marketing in this team is not to blame and is not a growth point for the business. The question arises: how to achieve the required contribution margin for this company? To find the optimal configuration, you need to apply Goldratt's approach to the entire economics: continuously look for bottlenecks and improve performance and by doing so arrive to the required contribution margin value, if it is possible.

UA	C1	B	AOV	COGS	APC	LTV	LTC	CM
15,000	1.57%	236	1,400.00	900.00	1.40	10.99	13.00	-30,150.00
15,000	1.57%	236	1,400.00	900.00	1.40	10.99	10.00	14,850.00
1,010,101	1.57%	15859	1,400.00	900.00	1.40	10.99	10.00	1,000,000.00
35,000	2.18%	761	1,600.00	860.00	1.91	30.68	2.11	1,000,000.00

So, we have reached the required value. At the same time, we had to optimize almost all the metrics available in the model, but the changes themselves are quite small.

Cohorts

Formation of cohorts

Now, it is time to deal with the error in the average payment count (APC), when the "Two Palms" team wrote 2 instead of 1.4. It may seem that such an error is a consequence of incorrect rounding: for example, they calculated that on average more than one box is purchased, which means there are two since part of the box cannot be purchased. But in fact, the mistake is much more complex — it plunges us into the world of cohort analysis, which is very important for product management and business in general.

The cohorts themselves appeared in business because there was a transition of the scaling unit from product to client and there was a need to take the client's economics over the course of his life into account in order to understand how effective this client was.

Let's start by defining a cohort. A cohort is a union of any objects according to predetermined characteristics. The cohort is formed over a period of time and then observed. The only quantity that does not change over time in a cohort is the number of objects that formed it. In unit economics, cohorts of scaling units (UA) are usually formed.

To understand how cohorts work, let's look at how they form over time.

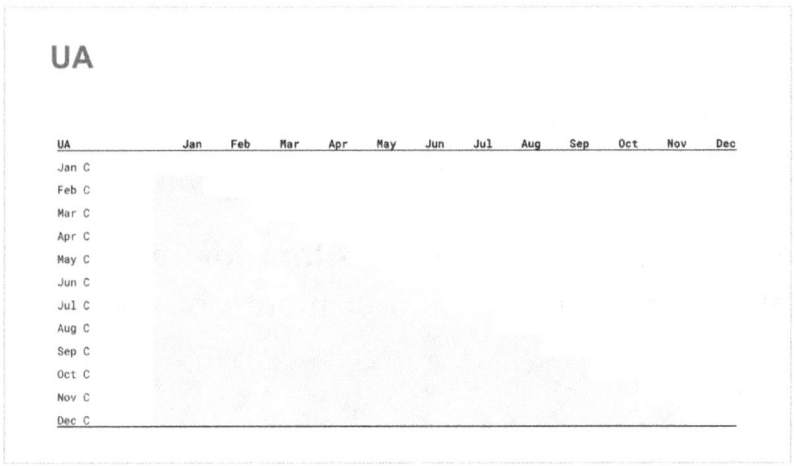

In the table below, the columns are months, ordinary time periods. The rows are cohorts of scaling units formed in specific months.

Let's say we launched a business in January, and this is the first month of work. We started the advertising campaign and attracted the first visitors, namely 15,000 visitors. We entered this value into the table, in the January column.

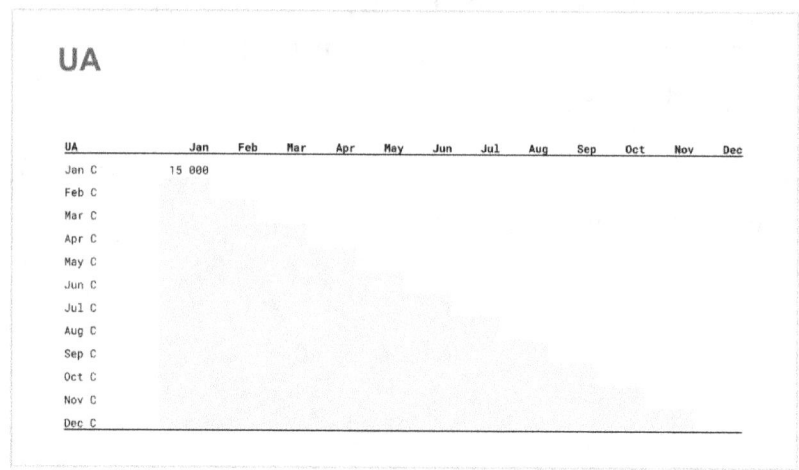

Since these are all our visitors for the current month and this is the first month of operation,

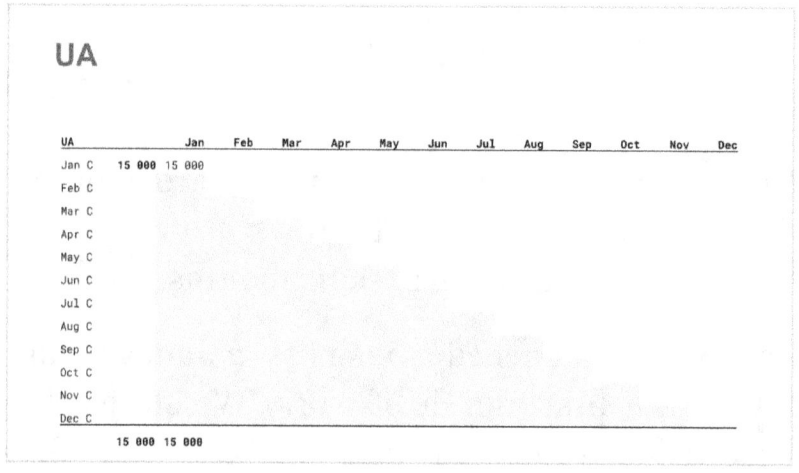

we fill in the cells on the left and below accordingly.

We will return to these values later. For now, let's see what happens to the cohorts next. In February, the advertising campaign continued, and new visitors who saw our project for the first time arrived. Since February is a short month, the figure was only 14,000. We enter this metric into the cells. Note that the cells at the bottom are summed across columns. We see that the January cohort has 15,000 visitors, and the February cohort - 14,000, with a total of 29,000 unique visitors over the two months.

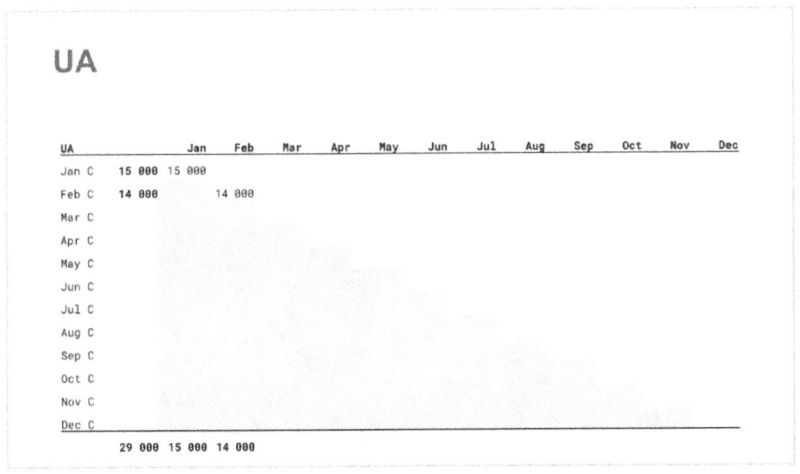

But those who have already visited us in January might have come back in February. So, in fact, part of the audience is the clients who returned to us. Let it be 7500 people. Let's enter this value in the February column, in the line of the January cohort. Please note that the number of visitors in the cohort does not change, since these are the same visitors as in January. But the number of visitors varies by month, and in February we already have 21,500 visitors, of which 14,000 are new, forming the February cohort, and 7,500 are from the previous month, belonging to the January cohort.

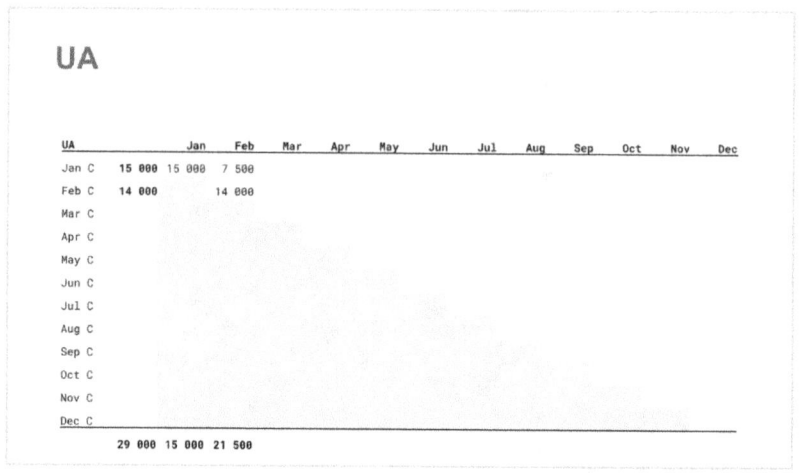

UA

UA	Jan	Feb	Mar	Apr	May	Jun	Jul	Aug	Sep	Oct	Nov	Dec
Jan C	15 000	15 000	7 500									
Feb C	14 000		14 000									
Mar C												
Apr C												
May C												
Jun C												
Jul C												
Aug C												
Sep C												
Oct C												
Nov C												
Dec C												
	29 000	15 000	21 500									

Next, we fill out the table for each month, highlighting new visitors who learned about the project for the first time and form a new cohort.

UA

UA		Jan	Feb	Mar	Apr	May	Jun	Jul	Aug	Sep	Oct	Nov	Dec
Jan C	15 000	15 000	7 500	3 750	1 875	938	469	234	189	190	221	167	143
Feb C	14 000		14 000	6 300	2 835	1 276	574	258	116	98	124	91	95
Mar C	13 000			13 000	3 900	1 170	351	105	32	9	3	1	1
Apr C	17 000				17 000	4 250	1 063	266	66	17	4	4	1
May C	18 000					18 000	3 600	720	144	29	6	5	3
Jun C	13 000						13 000	2 600	520	104	21	4	1
Jul C	15 000							15 000	3 000	600	120	24	5
Aug C	16 000								16 000	3 200	640	128	26
Sep C	15 000									15 000	3 000	600	120
Oct C	14 500										14 500	2 900	580
Nov C	16 000											16 000	3 200
Dec C	16 700												16 700
	183 200	15 000	21 500	23 050	25 610	25 634	19 057	19 183	20 067	19 247	18 639	19 924	20 875

Now let's see what happens to clients (for simplicity, let's make a reservation that in our model each client makes only one payment per month).

So, in January, when we launched the business, we had 15,000 visitors. Let 120 of them make a purchase immediately, in the first month. You can clearly see that the customer table is filled in the same way as we filled out the scaling units table.

UA → B

UA	Jan	Feb	Mar	Apr
Jan C	**15 000**	15 000		
Feb C				
Mar C				
Apr C				
May C				
Jun C				
Jul C				
Aug C				
Sep C				
Oct C				
Nov C				
Dec C				
	15 000	**15 000**		

B	Jan	Feb	Mar	Apr
Jan C	**120**	120		
Feb C				
Mar C				
Apr C				
May C				
Jun C				
Jul C				
Aug C				
Sep C				
Oct C				
Nov C				
Dec C				
	120	**120**		

In February, we had new visitors who were already forming their own cohort of scaling units. As we remember, there were 14,000 of them, and let 100 of them make a purchase in the first month, that is, in February. We enter these values into the table. So far everything is the same as it was with visitors.

UA → B

UA	Jan	Feb	Mar	Apr
Jan C	15 000	15 000		
Feb C	14 000		14 000	
Mar C				
Apr C				
May C				
Jun C				
Jul C				
Aug C				
Sep C				
Oct C				
Nov C				
Dec C				
	29 000	15 000	14 000	

B	Jan	Feb	Mar	Apr
Jan C	120	120		
Feb C	100		100	
Mar C				
Apr C				
May C				
Jun C				
Jul C				
Aug C				
Sep C				
Oct C				
Nov C				
Dec C				
	220	120	100	

We also remember that 7,500 visitors from the January cohort came in February, and let's imagine that 30 of them had also decided to buy the product. It means that in February we have 100 clients from the February cohort and 30 clients from the January cohort. Notice how the values in the first column of the client table have changed: there are now 150 clients in the January cohort.

UA → B

UA	Jan	Feb	Mar	Apr
Jan C	15 000	15 000	7 500	
Feb C	14 000		14 000	
Mar C				
Apr C				
May C				
Jun C				
Jul C				
Aug C				
Sep C				
Oct C				
Nov C				
Dec C				
	29 000	15 000	21 500	

B	Jan	Feb	Mar	Apr
Jan C	150	120	30	
Feb C	100		100	
Mar C				
Apr C				
May C				
Jun C				
Jul C				
Aug C				
Sep C				
Oct C				
Nov C				
Dec C				
	250	120	130	

We fill out the entire table of clients in the same way. It is important to remember that here we include only those customers who buy the product for the first time, since the scaling unit becomes a customer at the moment of making the first purchase.

It can be clearly seen that the January cohort contains 236 clients and they appeared throughout the 12 months. There are 199 clients in the February cohort, but they appeared throughout the 11 months and so on.

Клиенты (B)

B	Jan	Feb	Mar	Apr	May	Jun	Jul	Aug	Sep	Oct	Nov	Dec
Jan C	236	120	30	23	15	14	8	7	6	5	4	3	1
Feb C	199		100	45	20	10	9	5	4	3	1	1	1
Mar C	207			120	45	20	8	5	4	3	1	1	0
Apr C	257				150	50	30	13	6	4	3	1	0
May C	297					180	60	28	15	8	5	1	0
Jun C	173						120	28	13	7	3	1	1
Jul C	201							145	29	15	8	3	1
Aug C	280								170	50	35	15	10
Sep C	270									170	58	28	14
Oct C	254										180	50	24
Nov C	251											180	71
Dec C	242												242
	2 867	120	130	188	230	274	235	231	247	265	298	284	365

Now, it's time to figure out how to account for repeating sales that customers make. To do this, we need a third table — a table of transactions, or deals.

As we agreed above, each client makes no more than one transaction per month. This means that if we look at January, the transaction table is no different from the customer table.

UA → B → T

UA	Jan	Feb		B	Jan	Feb		T	Jan	Feb
Jan C	15 000	15 000		Jan C	120	120		Jan C	120	120
Feb C				Feb C				Feb C		
Mar C				Mar C				Mar C		
Apr C				Apr C				Apr C		
May C				May C				May C		
Jun C				Jun C				Jun C		
Jul C				Jul C				Jul C		
Aug C				Aug C				Aug C		
Sep C				Sep C				Sep C		
Oct C				Oct C				Oct C		
Nov C				Nov C				Nov C		
Dec C				Dec C				Dec C		
	15 000	15 000			120	120			120	120

Let's see what the transaction table will look like in February. If we consider only new visitors and new clients from February, then there are no changes.

UA → B → T

UA	Jan	Feb		B	Jan	Feb		T	Jan	Feb
Jan C	15 000	15 000		Jan C	120	120		Jan C	120	120
Feb C	14 000	14 000		Feb C	100	100		Feb C	100	100
Mar C				Mar C				Mar C		
Apr C				Apr C				Apr C		
May C				May C				May C		
Jun C				Jun C				Jun C		
Jul C				Jul C				Jul C		
Aug C				Aug C				Aug C		
Sep C				Sep C				Sep C		
Oct C				Oct C				Oct C		
Nov C				Nov C				Nov C		
Dec C				Dec C				Dec C		
	29 000	15 000	14 000		220	120	100		220	120	100

But we know that in February we had 7,500 visitors from the January cohort and 30 of them became clients. If you look at our table, there are 70 transactions noted. Where did another 40 additional transactions come from?

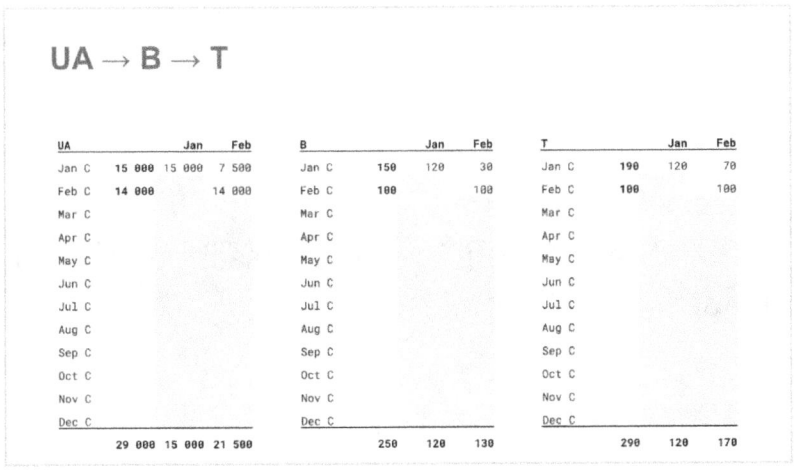

UA → B → T

UA		Jan	Feb
Jan C	15 000	15 000	7 500
Feb C	14 000		14 000
Mar C			
Apr C			
May C			
Jun C			
Jul C			
Aug C			
Sep C			
Oct C			
Nov C			
Dec C			
	29 000	15 000	21 500

B	Jan	Feb
Jan C	150	120	30
Feb C	100		100
Mar C			
Apr C			
May C			
Jun C			
Jul C			
Aug C			
Sep C			
Oct C			
Nov C			
Dec C			
	250	120	130

T	Jan	Feb
Jan C	190	120	70
Feb C	100		100
Mar C			
Apr C			
May C			
Jun C			
Jul C			
Aug C			
Sep C			
Oct C			
Nov C			
Dec C			
	290	120	170

Additional transactions appeared precisely due to the fact that customers of the January cohort, who bought the product in January, returned in February and made a repeating purchase. But of the 120 customers who appeared in January, only 40 returned. The rest have decided not to buy yet.

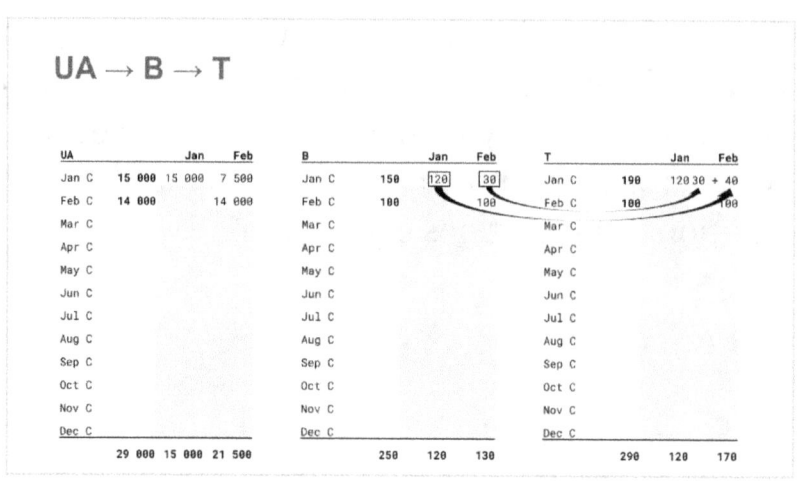

UA → B → T

We continue to fill in the transaction table by analogy with other tables.

Transactions (T)

T		Jan	Feb	Mar	Apr	May	Jun	Jul	Aug	Sep	Oct	Nov	Dec
Jan C	1 083	120	70	72	74	78	82	87	94	97	100	104	105
Feb C	664		100	65	50	45	40	38	35	70	72	74	75
Mar C	232			120	50	30	15	7	4	3	1	1	1
Apr C	294				150	60	45	20	6	4	4	4	1
May C	306					180	62	29	15	9	6	3	2
Jun C	176						120	29	14	7	4	1	1
Jul C	203							145	30	15	9	3	1
Aug C	283								170	51	35	16	11
Sep C	273									170	58	30	15
Oct C	256										180	52	24
Nov C	252											180	72
Dec C	242												242
	4 264	120	170	257	324	393	364	355	368	426	469	468	550

The importance of cohorts

As a matter of fact, these manipulations are enough to understand how the team made a mistake with the average payment count. In addition, we will see that the cohort approach allows us to see such errors in advance and avoid serious problems in the business.

To calculate the average average payment count, you need to divide the number of transactions by the number of clients. To understand how many clients there were in the cohort, you need to know the number of scaling units and the conversion rate.

As a result, we will get the following table, in which each column contains the value of a particular metric in the cohort corresponding to the column.

In January, we formed a cohort of 15,000 scaling units that added 236 clients within 12 months. These customers completed 1,083 transactions over a 12-month period. Thus, the conversion rate in the cohort over 12 months is 1.57%, and the average number of transactions per customer is 4.59.

	Jan C	Feb C	Mar C	Apr C	May C	Jun C	Jul C	Aug C	Sep C	Oct C	Nov C	Dec C	Average	Total
UA	15 000	14 000	13 000	17 000	18 000	13 000	15 000	16 000	15 000	14 500	16 000	16 700	15 267	183 200
C_1	1.57%	1.42%	1.59%	1.51%	1.65%	1.33%	1.34%	1.75%	1.80%	1.75%	1.57%	1.45%	1.56%	1.56%
B	236	199	207	257	297	173	201	280	270	254	251	242	239	2 867
T	1 083	664	232	294	306	176	203	283	273	256	252	242	355	4 264
APC	4.59	3.34	1.12	1.14	1.03	1.02	1.01	1.01	1.01	1.01	1.00	1.00	1.52	1.49

February is a shorter month and, in addition, the cohort formed in February lived one month less than the January one (11 months). Out of 14,000 scaling units, the output was 199 clients and 664 transactions. The conversion rate is 1.42%, and the average payment count is 3.34.

And so on, until December. The December cohort lived only one month. We have 242 clients who made 242 transactions. On average, there is one transaction per client.

Now, we need to find out what the average payment count was for the entire year. This indicator can be calculated in two ways. The first is to take the average number of deals from each cohort, add those values upfor the year and divide by 12. We get the APC value shown in the first column after the table, called Average: 1.52.

The second way is to add up all transactions for the year and divide by the number of all clients for the year. We get 1.49 — this number is indicated in the second column after the table, called Total.

We took the same data set, worked with it differently and got completely different results. A reasonable question arises: which method is correct and how to use all this in business?

If we correct the mistake that the "Two Palms" team made, then we must proceed the second way. Namely, we should take the total number of clients and transactions for the year since we are interested in the average payment count for the entire time.

However, for a business, calculating the average number of transactions is useful in both ways. The point is that the difference between these two values indicates how loyal the client is.

If we look at the table carefully, we will see that the average number of transactions for the first cohort is 4.59, for the second — 3.34 and for the last — 1.00. Therefore, in March we could have expected 3.00 or 2.90, but we got 1.12. This suggests that there were some changes in the business this month that led to a sharp drop in customer return.

But could this be seen if we looked at the business in the traditional way, simply by monthly metrics?

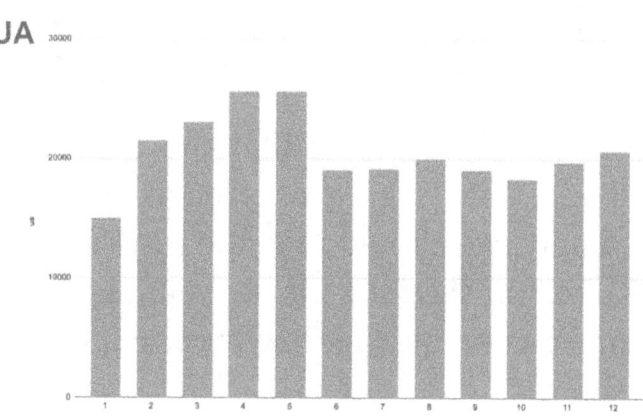

The number of visitors generally increases evenly from month to month. After May, a slight decline is visible, but then there is an upward trend.

So, everything goes well concerning the clients, there is a clear growth trend.

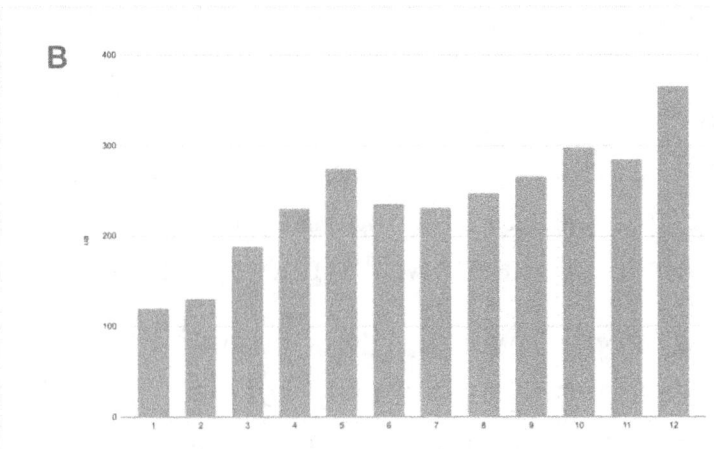

Transactions are also growing.

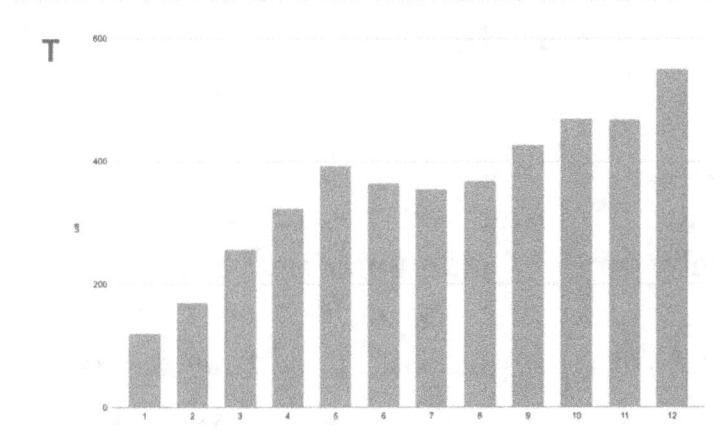

But, as we see in the cohorts, user loyalty fell in March. And taking into account the fact that the unit economics of the business turned out to be negative, the average payment count is an important parameter. At the current indicator reflected in the example, the business goes bankrupt. This can only be seen during the analysis of the cohorts. Moreover, it was possible to pay attention to this issue already in April, and not later when the growth of new clients stopped.

Unit economics works with a potential or actual client as a scaling unit in cohorts. This has obvious benefits, but it also makes life a little more difficult when working with financial modeling.

Time in cohorts

In order to better understand the structure of cohorts, it is necessary to become familiar with another important feature of cohort analysis, namely time. Communicating with business representatives, I regularly encountered diffi-culties with the perception of time in cohorts. The fact is that we are accustomed to thinking about time as an interval that we are currently studying. Namely: how our balance changed over the past month, what it was like two months ago, and so on. However, cohorts work a little differently.

To understand time in cohorts, you need to start by finding the right business question to help you understand this concept. When you ask yourself what your balance was last month, you just want information about money. But knowing that number, you likely won't be able to answer why it is that way or what you need to do to improve it.

Of course, you can say that you just need to sell more, but it's important to understand to whom: old clients or new ones? If new, then how much will it cost to find them? And how much money will be spent on selling to the old ones? To get the right answer, you need to start asking yourself what sales did the clients we attracted, for example, in January last year bring in last month? And how many sales during the same period were brought by the clients we attracted in February last year, and so on. In fact, the question comes down to how our sales are structured in the context of the period of attracting customers who made these sales.

Actually, we are already gradually getting acquainted with the time in cohorts: we have the time of cohort formation - this is the time during which a cohort of clients was formed, and the time at which we look at the value of any indicators associated with the cohort.

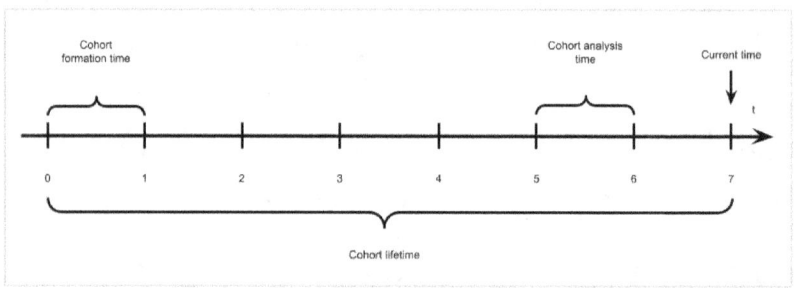

The figure shows a time scale on which equal intervals are displayed, let these be months. The first interval is the time during which a cohort, for example, clients, was formed. This means that all new clients during this interval are marked as belonging to this cohort. Next is the current time, that is, the time in which the researcher who wants to gain an understanding of what is happening with the indicators of his business is located. In the diagram, he is on the border of the 7th interval. At the same time, he wants to understand what volume of sales was made by clients from the first cohort, formed in the first time interval, during the previous to the current interval, namely the 6th interval. At the same time, we know that in the 7th time interval, clients from this cohort have already made purchases, and therefore are active at the moment. This means that we can say that a cohort formed in the first interval has a lifetime equal to 7 intervals.

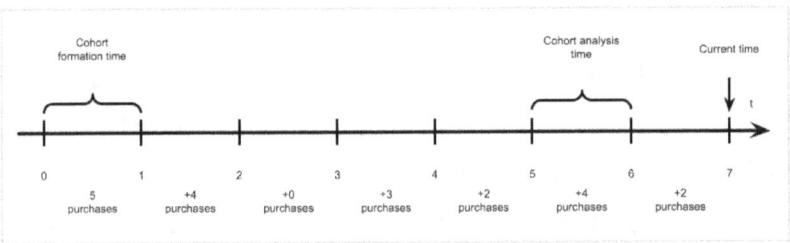

Let's look at why time works the way it does in cohorts and why it's important. Let us have one cohort formed during the first time interval. Moreover, during the same time interval clients included in this cohort made 5 purchases. In the next interval — 4 additional purchases; after another interval, clients in the cohort rested and did not make purchases. In the fourth interval, customers returned and made 3 additional purchases, and in the next interval they made 2 additional purchases. In the sixth interval that is being studied there were 4 more additional purchases and, finally, in the last interval, at the current moment, there are two more additional purchases.

Please, note that the clients from this cohort are currently active, which means that the lifetime of the cohort is equal to the time that has passed from the moment of its formation to the current moment, inclusive.

If you ask how many sales this cohort brought in during the period of time under study — in interval 6 — then the answer is 4. But at the same time, clients of the same cohort from the moment of formation until the study period inclusive made 16 purchases. And for the entire life of the cohort — 18.

What can this knowledge give us? In previous chapters, I've shown why it's important to look at economic performance across cohorts. In fast-growing companies and startups, it's easy to miss dramatic changes in the customer experience, leading to wasted money, cash gaps, and so on.

Therefore, when you work with unit economics metrics, it is very important to understand what time period of the cohort life we are talking about: it might be the formation time, or the lifetime, or some specific interval during the lifetime, or from the moment of foundation to the interval under study. In all the cases, you may get different values.

Accordingly, comparing metrics from different cohorts, it is important to check that the time of formation of the cohort is the same. If one cohort was formed within a month, then the second should also be formed within the same period.

Strictly speaking, all metrics in unit economics must have the same dimension so that cohorts can be effectively compared with each other. For example, you use a subscription monetization model and you have two tariff plans: the first one costs 100 rubles per month and the second costs 1000 rubles, but for a year. If we take only two clients who purchased one of these tariff plans each, then formally we have two payments, one for 100 rubles and the one for 1000 rubles. And it may seem that the average check here is calculated simply as

$$(100 + 1000) / 2 = 550$$

However, this is incorrect, because clients paid for different periods of use of the service: the first one paid only for one month, the second bought

12 months at once. Therefore, it would be correct to standardize payments. It is most convenient to do this for a month. Then we get that the first client paid for one month 100 rubles, and the second — 12 times in total for 1000 rubles. And then the average check will be calculated according to the formula

$$(100 + 83.3(3) \times 12) / 13 \approx 84.62$$

You must agree that this changes the value of the average check greatly. In addition, the frequency of payments also changes. There will be not one, but

$$(1 + 12) / 2 = 6.5$$

That is, two clients made 13 payments.

Startup financial model

Why do you need a financial model?

Working with startups, I often came across the question of why an entrepreneur needs to create a financial model and generally describe a business plan. There is an opinion that innovative startups should not create their own model and business plan during the early stages. I admit, I don't know where this came from, but I've heard it many times, not only from startup founders, but also from various participants of the venture ecosystem: consultants, experts, VC partners and even investors.

However, all this, of course, is not entirely correct. As I see, the main problem is that the founders of innovative startups often do not have experience working with such documents and do not understand how to create them. These documents look very complex and, while working with them, the innovator needs to have an understanding of a very large amount of data describing everything: the market in which the product will operate, the project team, the client, and the basic characteristics of the product. But since very often innovators are in a hurry to implement their idea, they simply do not have time to properly prepare for work.

As a result, when the time comes, they prepare a document, by hook or by crook, that, naturally, has nothing to do with reality and is almost never implemented as a result. That is, if the entrepreneur manages to receive investments using such a document at all. Apparently, due to the fact that such plans for the most part are not implemented, the opinion has spread that there is no need for such a document. But this is just my guess.

So, why does an entrepreneur need a financial model? The main purpose of the model is to make sure that he clearly understands what he wants to do, what resources he must spend, what product characteristics he must achieve and what profit he plans to receive. In addition, such models make it possible to evaluate the investment attractiveness of a project, assess the volume of required investments and check whether the entrepreneur understands the operation of his future product correctly.

When an entrepreneur comes to an investor and presents his idea, the investor is interested, among other things, in how much money is needed for its implementation, how this money is planned to be spent and what effect will be from it, when one should expect profit, how long it will take for the investor to return the invested money in dividends or through the sale of shares. A financial model helps answer all these questions.

However, most startups, especially beginners, do not understand this approach and prepare documents based on insufficiently correct information. For example, an early seed investment fund announces a selection of startups for investment and offers for a small share, about 5-10%, to provide investments with a fixed valuation of the startup, for example, $1,000,000 for the duration of an acceleration program lasting 6 months. If we assume that the share will be 5%, then the fund gives the startup $50,000 for 6 months.

Startups submit applications, and in these applications, they do not write the actual required amount of investment, but set a precise amount — $50,000. They adjust their models to this value and for this reason they look unrealistic, many things do not fit together. Though, a startup must understand that it may be unprofitable for a fairly long period of time and, therefore, it will have to attract investments more than once. The current early-stage venture fund will only be the first among all investors in the project.

Also, an investor looks at the financial model in order to see how the startup plans to grow. Namely: how the value that the startup creates will change, how its capitalization and audience will change.

This is necessary in order to assess the investment potential for the subsequent return of your money.

For example, if an investor understands that the startup offered to him for investment plans to grow by expanding its users, then a 20-fold increase in the audience over two years can significantly increase the capitalization of the business, even if it does not have time to pass the break-even point during this time — the main thing is that those parameters that interest the investor grow.

Traditionally, it is assumed that, within a clear planning horizon, a startup will be able to bring the unit economics of its product to positive values and ensure a sufficient increase in the number of scaling units while the final profit may remain negative.

A financial model can also be applied to the analysis of business development using the plan-fact approach. In this analysis, an entrepreneur, having agreed on a model and launched a business, begins to keep records of actual indicators and then, once in a specific period, checks the compliance of the planned values of the model with the actual ones. It allows one to make quick management decisions that help the company reach economic targets.

This approach allows the investor not to risk the entire amount of the required investment, but to divide it into tranches and invest in the project in parts checking the deviation of the actual business indicators from the planned ones.

All this suggests that the financial model is a fairly important document that you need to learn how to prepare. And unit economics is one of the tools that allows you to do this quite easily. All you have to do is to follow some rules of creating such a document.

The structure of the financial model

First, let's figure out what is a profit and loss statement, or, simply, P&L. It is one of the three main financial documents adopted as a management reporting standard, such as the profit and loss statement, cash flow statement and balance sheet. But it is important to note that we will not talk about the report itself focusing on the model version of the P&L, since the purpose of the book is to prepare entrepreneurs for working with such documents. We are talking about startups and enterprises at the very beginning of their journey.

In general, I prefer to divide such documents into three types. The first is the report itself collected on the basis of current sales and expenses. It is built on the basis of real data obtained. The second is predictive, built on the basis of historical data. The value of indicators in the future is predicted taking into account their behavior in the past. The third one is the one we will talk about — a model report that is created from scratch. Its task is to show what a business should be like in order to meet the tasks set for it by the founders, investors and the team.

The document itself looks quite simple: it is a table in which the rows are items of income and expenses, and the columns are periods, usually months. The cells contain values. What needs to be shown to the investor is what the income will be in each period of the plan and what the expenses will be. This is a general part, but in reality, an investor will want to see the detailed information not only about the way your income will be generated, but also about the way the money will be spent. Therefore, it is important to display these parts correctly.

Since we will be working with modeling the P&L statement and doing this using unit economics, let me tell you about my vision of the structure of such documents.

Let's note that the logic of the document is to show the difference between the income and expenses, which, in fact, is one of the types of profit, namely EBITDA, or earnings before interest, taxes, depreciation and amortization. As we remember from the first chapters, this is the difference between contribution margin and fixed costs. Therefore, we need to start by showing how we generate our income using the contribution margin structure. That is, we will show what the unit economics of our business looks like.

In addition, unit economics will answer the question of how much money the project plans to earn in a specific period. Next, we just have to write down our fixed costs and get the EBITDA value for each period.

Let's look at a template for such a plan using the example of a service that works on a subscription basis with individuals. Let it be a solution for learning foreign languages – "Do you speak English?" that sells English language courses through an application. It uses a simple subscription model and has two pricing plans:

monthly for \$10 and annual for 12 months at \$80.

But before showing the structure of the unit economics, let's make a small digression and remember that the unit economics of the business with the client as the scaling unit has a cohort essence. That is, all metric values relate to the lifetime of the cohort and it will differ from the periods during which we create our document. "Do you speak English?" makes a subscription product and expects that the customers will use it for quite a long time. And this is definitely more than one or even several months. Thus, in each period of the plan we must display both new customers and visitors and the old ones who are already using the product.

We will find out how to do this later, for now we will take into account the fact that we will have new unit economics metrics that were not previously mentioned or used, namely: ua_{new}, ua_{old}, ua_{churn} and ua_{total} and, accordingly, b_{new}, b_{old}, b_{churn} and b_{total}. The first group describes cohorts for service visitors, the second — for clients. NEW means new for the period, OLD means old, CHURN is the number lost in the period relative to the previous period, and TOTAL is the total number of users or clients in the period. In order to find these values, we will need additional parameters, such as the amount of outflow or return RR and CR. The first — to account for the return of visitors, the second — to account for the outflow of customers.

	A	B
1		
2	UNIT-ECONOMICS	
3	**Leads**	
4	new (ua)	
5	old	
6	churn	
7	total	
8		
9	**Product**	
10	C1	
11	COGS	
12	APC	
13	RR, leads	
14	CR, customer	
15	CAC	
16	CPA	
17		
18	**Customers**	
19	Customers, new (b)	
20	Customers,old	
21	Customers, churn	
22	Customers, total	
23		
24	INCOME	
25		
26	EXPENSES	
27		
28	RESULTS	

Let's look at the structure of the document. So far, we have filled out the first part, the description of the product and unit economics. The next step is to describe the income. In general, this part is quite simple: you need to show what the project's average check will be in each period and, accordingly, the total income from all sales. If a business has several different products, then you can make the average bill and income for each product separately and then add the amount from all the products. In our example, we do not assume separation by tariff plans; there will simply be one average check for the entire product.

Next comes the expenses, and this is a very important section. Startups often treat it very carelessly and enter only some basic expenses forgetting to mention important types of necessary expenses.

Another difficulty is caused by the need to create dynamic fixed costs that depend on the number of clients or are somehow related to other plan parameters. For example, "Do you speak English?" is going to purchase servers for its work depending on how many users the service will have. In addition, the number of support staff will depend directly on the number of service clients.

For simplicity, we will limit ourselves to three types of fixed costs: wages, rent and other expenses summed up and included in the "other" item of expense. Variable costs consist of COGS costs and the costs of attracting and retaining potential customers. The total amount of all costs is entered in the total line.

28	EXPENSES
29	**Variable costs**
30	COGS
31	Advertaizing costs, new
32	Advertaizing costs, old
33	
34	**Fixed Costs**
35	Salary
36	Rent
37	Other
38	
39	**Total**

In the last section (results), we place the minimum set of indicators necessary to assess the effectiveness of the selected model — gross profitability, contribution margin, EBITDA, taxes, profit and cumulative profit. This is the minimum set that will allow you to create a model.

40	
41	RESULTS
42	Gross Margin
43	Contribution Margin
44	
45	EBITDA
46	TAX
47	
48	PROFIT
49	CUMULATIVE PROFIT
50	

The next step is to enter the values of the model during the period when the first sales are made. What period is this? If you are creating a complex innovative product, then you will spend some time developing it. Let's say it will be 6 months before the first working version is released. During this time you will have expenses, but no income.

Since the project is quite simple in its initial state, we will assume that it will take three months to prepare for sales. To launch the product, a mobile application and a web service, we will need a small team of two server-side developers and two application developers: one will create the mobile app, the other will create the web version. The team will also need a methodologist who will develop methods and lessons, and since this is a fairly large task, there will be 3 of them. The founder of the product will play two roles at once, CEO and CPO, and the second founder will be responsible for marketing. In addition, he should also be assisted by a traffic specialist. And the last person on the team will be a support employee. So, it is 11 people in total.

The total labor costs for our team will be 1,450,000 rubles including taxes per month. The team will also have to rent a coworking space, which will cost 165,000 rubles per month. We estimate all other expenses — Internet, hosting, telephony, etc. — at another 15,000 rubles. Then the table will look like this:

34	**Fixed Costs**			
35	Salary	1,450,000.00	1,450,000.00	1,450,000.00
36	Rent	165,000.00	165,000.00	165,000.00
37	Other	15,000.00	15,000.00	15,000.00
38				
39	**Total**	1,630,000.00	1,630,000.00	1,630,000.00
40				
41	RESULTS			
42	Gross Margin	0.00	0.00	0.00
43	Contribution Margin	0.00	0.00	0.00
44				
45	EBITDA	-1,630,000.00	-1,630,000.00	-1,630,000.00
46	TAX	0.00	0.00	0.00
47				
48	PROFIT	-1,630,000.00	-1,630,000.00	-1,630,000.00
49	CUMULATIVE PROFIT	-1,630,000.00	-3,260,000.00	-4,890,000.00
50				

Starting from the fourth month, the company plans to earn money. Therefore, the team needs to understand what metrics the product will meet in the first month of sales. This is a non-trivial question: essentially, you need to imagine how many potential clients you can attract in the first month, what the conversion rate will be, and so on. Here we will consider the case when sales begin in the first month, but it is important to understand that in reality, a longer period may pass before the first sales.

I entered the indicators for the first month based on the assumption that the team would be able to attract 1000 potential clients to the site at a price of 50 rubles each and achieve a conversion of 0.4%.

In order to fill the table out, you need to calculate the average check. We know that the project will have two payment options: a subscription with a monthly charge of $10 and with an annual charge of $80 paid for 12 months. To understand what the average check will be for this project, you need to assume how subscriptions will be distributed among clients, what percentage of clients will choose to pay monthly and what percentage will choose to pay immediately for the year.

When a startup is just launching, it is correct to assume that the number of subscribers who will immediately choose an annual plan will be fewer than those who will choose a monthly subscription. Why is it so? While there is no trust in the product, people will be interested in the opportunity to unsubscribe from the project and savings will not be a priority. But over time, when users understand that the product is of a good quality, customers will switch from monthly tariff plans to annual ones. So, let's assume that in the first month only 5% of customers choose the annual plan. Then, the average check can be calculated using the formula:

$$AOV = 10 \times 95\% + (80/12) \times 5\% = 9.83$$

in this case, the average payment count will be calculated as:

$$APC = 0.95 + 12 \times 0.05 = 1.55$$

Let me explain what operations I performed. Since only 5% buy the annual tariff, you need to convert the price paid by such clients to a monthly payment first. To do this, we divide it by 12, and then multiply it by the share of such clients. We do the same with the number of payments: those who choose a one-time subscription have one payment by default, and those who paid for the year at once receive 12 payments. Note that all this applies specifically to the first month of sales.

	A	B	C	D	E
1		1.2022	2.2022	3.2022	4.2022
2	UNIT-ECONOMICS				
3	Leads				
4	new (ua)				1,000
5	old				0
6	churn				0
7	total				1,000
8					
9	Product				
10	C1				0.40%
11	COGS				23.59
12	APC				1.55
13	RR, leads				50.00%
14	CR, customer				64.52%
15	CAC				12,500.00
16	CPA				50.00
17					
18	Customers				
19	Customers, new (b)				4
20	Customers, old				0
21	Customers, churn				0
22	Customers, total				4
23					
24	INCOME				
25	Average Order Value (AOV)				786.40
26	Revenue				3,145.60
27					
28	EXPENSES				
29	Variable costs				
30	COGS				94.37
31	Advertaizing costs, new				50,000.00
32	Advertaizing costs, old				0.00
33					
34	Fixed Costs				
35	Salary	1,450,000.00	1,450,000.00	1,450,000.00	1,450,000.00
36	Rent	165,000.00	165,000.00	165,000.00	165,000.00
37	Other	15,000.00	15,000.00	15,000.00	15,000.00
38					
39	Total	1,630,000.00	1,630,000.00	1,630,000.00	1,680,094.37
40					
41	RESULTS				
42	Gross Margin	0.00	0.00	0.00	3,051.23
43	Contribution Margin	0.00	0.00	0.00	-46,948.77
44					
45	EBITDA	-1,630,000.00	-1,630,000.00	-1,630,000.00	-1,676,948.77
46	TAX	0.00	0.00	0.00	0.00
47					
48	PROFIT	-1,630,000.00	-1,630,000.00	-1,630,000.00	-1,676,948.77
49	CUMULATIVE PROFIT	-1,630,000.00	-3,260,000.00	-4,890,000.00	-6,566,948.77
50					

The price has also been converted into rubles for ease of calculation. As the team's expenses are calculated in rubles, it is better to calculate income in the same currency, even if the actual sales will take place in a different currency.

Now, it's time to decide what the company wants to achieve with this business: what is the final goal. To begin with, let us note that the business has fixed costs, and they amount to a total of 1,630,000 rubles per month.

As we remember, unit economics is the determination of the number of scaling units, the contribution margin from which is necessary to cover fixed costs and reach a given profit level. If a company wants to reach 10,000,000 rubles in contribution margin, then, maintaining current expenses, it can count on approximately 8,400,000 rubles in profit.

The next important question that needs to be answered is what period the company wants (and, most importantly, is ready) to devote to achieving this result. Since we are talking about a startup, we will focus on three years. This means that the team has only 36 months, of which the first three will be spent on development and the remaining 33 — on sales and improvement.

Using unit economics and the Goldratt approach, you can find the cohort value at which the business will reach the specified indicators – 10,000,000 rubles in contribution margin.

UA	C1	B	AOV	COGS	APC	LTV	LTC	CM
1,000	0.40%	4	786.48	23.59	1.55	4.73	50.00	-45,270.58
150,000	1.82%	2730	786.48	23.59	6.96	96.63	30.00	10,000,000.00

It is clearly seen that almost all unit economic indicators will have to be improved. All we have to do is to figure out how to do this within a given period. You need to fill the model out and indicate how each metric will change from month to month.

Before entering data into cells, you need to understand what type of growth is expected from period to period. In my work with startups, I have often seen the use of linear growth. In this case, a certain time interval is taken, divided into steps (periods) and then the difference in metrics between the final and initial values is divided by the number of steps. The result is the value of growth for each step.

For example, UA at the start is 1000 and at the finish – 60,000, the number of periods is 33 (out of 36 months of planning, the company spends three months preparing and not selling the product). The grows of the indicator from month to month will be calculated using the formula:

$$\Delta = \frac{UA_{end} - UA_{start}}{N-1} = \frac{60\,000 - 1000}{32} = 1843.75$$

This approach is chosen because it is easiest to implement by modeling metrics. But it has a big drawback: it requires constant growth by an even amount, starting from the first month. But if a startup grows quickly, then the increase from the first month turns out to be very significant. In this case, a smooth growth will be practically unattainable.

An alternative type of growth is exponential: when the growth is small at first, but increases over time and allows you to reach the specified values.

$$\Delta = \frac{UA_{end}}{UA_{strat}}^{\frac{1}{N-1}}$$

Unlike the linear growth formula, the delta here is multiplied by the previous value. So, if you wish, you can build a model that will use both options.

If we generally understand the growth of metrics, then we just have to figure out how to calculate cohort indicators, such as UA and B, from period to period. That is, how to account for the client churn.

The first thing to remember is that potential clients come and go in different ways than the real ones. It means that churn and return models for each type of clients must be created separately.

In the case of real clients, this parameter is determined by the unit economics itself, namely:

$$CR = \frac{1}{APC}$$

The client churn rate is inversely proportional to the average number of payments for the cohort. It's important to note that this is more or less relevant for a subscription model, but when it comes to e-commerce, it's not so simple.

Essentially, this approach assumes that the client base decreases evenly, with the same amount; at the same time, in e-commerce, client churn and return are more random.

In this case, we will choose this approach for two reasons. Firstly, we assume that the business in our model should grow and, therefore, we consider the outflow to be minimal and uniform. Secondly, we are not really talking about e-commerce here. One way or another, our task is in each period to take account of the potential and actual clients from previous periods. Solving it requires either a detailed immersion in working with tables or the use of special software to create a model profit and loss plan. In general, the plan will look like this:

Of course, the format of such documents means that they should be viewed on a computer screen, in spreadsheet applications like Excel or Google Spreadsheet.

What is important here is that this table was created without much effort, by answering questions about the team's ability to achieve indicators through its competencies. And this, in turn, allows the founder to understand how to assemble a team and what specialists to hire.

How a startup grows

In its financial model, a company must show growth from period to period. For example, it should grow by 20% over the year or show 15% month-to-month growth if it is a startup. These figures are very arbitrary and, when creating financial models, the founders often do not understand how to set the growth of indicators so that it looks realistic. After all, all metrics are interconnected and a change in one entails a change in others.

To solve this problem, let's first understand what growth can be like. There are many methods for changing metrics over time, but let's consider three of them here: linear, exponential, and sigmoid. At the same time, in real financial models that startups create, I see either a linear or a stepwise method that is not considered here.

The reason for using them is simple: they are quite easy to create in tables with minimal knowledge of mathematics. With the exponential, and even more so with the sigmoid, everything is much more complicated.

To understand this, let's look at the "physical meaning" of these types of growth. Since a startup is a project implemented in conditions of uncertainty and lack of competencies, it cannot grow with a sharp spurt. It grows smoothly, gradually increasing its growth. And this type of growth is described by an exponential.

A sigmoid is a special type of curve that is characterized by three growth areas: first there is a smooth increase in the characteristic, then a sharp increase begins, and after that the increase is smooth again. This is how the characteristics become saturated and the metric approaches a certain peak value.

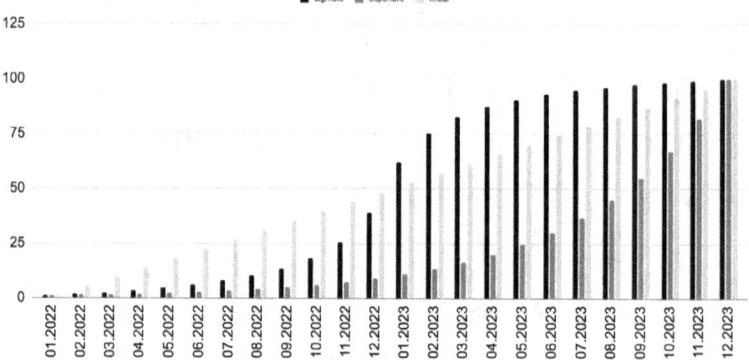

In this figure, blue shows sigmoid growth, red shows exponential growth and yellow shows linear growth. And it is very clear how the characteristic must change in order to reach the final value within a given time interval.

To create a simple model at the stage of the first investment for initial assessment, I recommend using exponential growth of metrics. And if the project is faced with the task of building a plan for several stages of investment (for example, three) while the modeling period is about five years, then you can use sigmoid growth of metrics for each stage. We will discuss it in the following parts of the book This is somewhat more difficult to implement, but it is quite possible. Especially if you use ready-made templates[14].

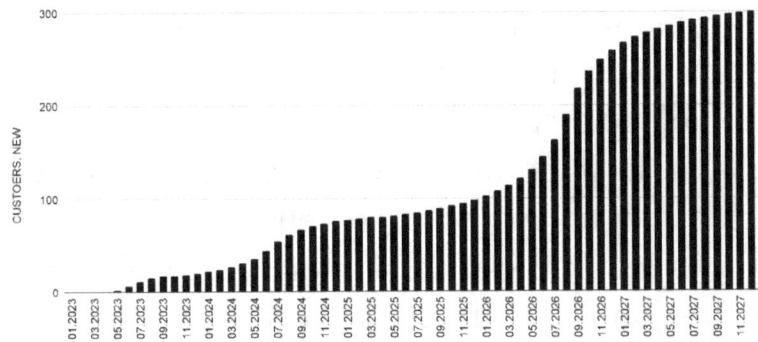

The figure clearly shows three areas of growth in the number of new clients that correspond to three different stages of investment. At the same time, the team understands that with each stage it will approach some saturation, and part of the investment will be used to begin a new growth through strengthening competencies. At the same time, the sigmoid is designed in such a way that the growth occurs exponentially. This meets the expectations about the way the startup indicators should grow.

---

[14] https://khanin.info/templates/saas-sigmoid

Evaluation of a startup's investment potential

It's time to deal with one of the main tasks for which a startup's financial model is created — the task of attracting investments. Moreover, this task is so important and at the same time difficult for novice entrepreneurs to understand that in real life you encounter completely inexplicable applications for investments from the startups.

The requested amounts generally come down to some random number that has nothing to do with the real needs of the team and correlates only with the personal desires of the founders to receive money or take exactly as much as the investor offers. Both options are unacceptable and the likelihood of receiving money is minimal here.

As we remember, in the chapter "What is unit economics?", I defined investments as the money that covers the difference between contribution margin and fixed costs. This essentially means that the money is used to cover the company's losses until it passes the break-even point. In reality, there is still a need to cover all variable costs: the fact is that these costs must be faced before the business receives money from the client, and, therefore, the startup must have the means to cover them.

In general, I suggest estimating the amount of investment required at least by the amount of the ideal loss, taking into account the break-even points and, ideally, the variable costs, in particular marketing expenses.

At the same time, you should not be afraid that creating a model for the period of 5 years, you will face the total investments amounting to tens of millions of rubles or even dollars, while the break-even point will be reached after three or even four years of work. There is no need to be afraid of this, because it takes serious effort to start any business and an innovative one requires even more energy.

However, early-stage startups are faced with the question of how to apply for acceleration programs for three to six months in which they plan to receive small investments of two or three million rubles, while showing a financial model in which the amount of investment required is, for example, 15 million? This situation occurs quite often among startups, but it has a very simple solution: you need to explain to the investor that 15 million rubles are required for implementation of this project for a period of 5 years and the team is considering several stages of investment. The first stage will last, for example, 6 months and will require 4 million rubles.

Next, the team should look at the product metrics in the model that should be achieved over this period, and justify that it is realistic to achieve these values. These very indicators, in turn, are a kind of criteria for the investor to continue working with the startup and providing it with the next round of investment.

In order to look at a more realistic situation, it is recommended to draw up a so-called capitalization table. In such a table, it is important to note all the investors and owners of shares in the shared capital and indicate the periods of investment, shares and capitalization of the company. In a simplified form, such a table might look like this:

	Foundation	Stage 1	Stage 2	Stage 3
founders	100.00%	90.00%	76.50%	57.38%
investors		10.00%	8.50%	6.38%
investors			15.00%	11.25%
investors				25.00%
FOUNDERS	Share	Stage 1	Stage 2	Stage 3
founder 1	90.00%	81.00%	68.85%	51.64%
founder 2	10.00%	9.00%	7.65%	5.74%
STAGE 1				
Investor 1	5%	5.00%	4.25%	3.19%
Investor 2	5%	5.00%	4.25%	3.19%
STAGE 2				
Investor 1	10%		10.00%	7.50%
Investor 2	5%		5.00%	3.75%
STAGE 3				
Investor 1	20%			20.00%
Investor 2	5%			5.00%

From the table above, it is clear that the startup has three rounds of investment. Each round involves two investors (6 in total) and two startup founders. In each round, the shares of all shareholders were diluted in order to distribute the share to new investors. As a result, it can be seen that, based on the results of three rounds, the first founder firmly retains control over the company, but his share falls from 90% of the profitability to 51.64%, while the main investor of the third round with shares of 20% becomes the second decision-maker in the business.

The values of marketing costs and EBITDA are calculated for each round separately. If EBITDA is negative, only this value is taken into account in calculation of investment. If EBITDA becomes positive (passing the break-even point), then only marketing costs are taken into account in calculation of investments.

As a result, working with such a model, an entrepreneur and an investor immediately see what investments are actually required in the project, when the break-even point is planned to be reached, what the investments will be spent on, and what parameters the startup must achieve in order to fulfill the stated plan. This means that it is possible to plan the stages of investment and, in general, the investor's work with a startup becomes more transparent.

Building models for complex businesses

In the last chapter, I would like to talk about a situation in which you need to create a financial model for a business that has several different products and types of customers. This is not a very common situation among novice entrepreneurs, but quite experienced entrepreneurs face such cases.

Let's imagine a startup: a team is developing a certain technological platform that solves the problems of individuals who use a subscription service at a low cost — b2c business. At the same time, there are large companies on the market that can also provide relevant services to these same individuals. And our startup sells various information about its users to these companies - now, this is a b2b business.

At the same time, we have one technology platform that is made by one team producing two completely different products with different sales teams and different presentation strategies. It turns out that we need to calculate two different unit economics and build two different financial models, which then need to be combined into one, because the business is the same.

In this example, the solution is obvious and simple: unit economics is built for each business separately and is used to build the revenue part of the financial model. The expense part common to both businesses is compiled separately, since there is actually one team.

But there are also more complex examples in which the created product is single, but the offers made to the same audience are different. For example, you can buy a subscription to watch films in an online cinema or you can pay in order to watch a specific film once. Thus, some people buy a one-time viewing, and others buy a subscription. At the same time, the marketing for both variants is the same, dividing the audience is not easy. And there are two obviously different products with their own unit economics model each.

The difficulty of this model is that in unit economics it is difficult to separate potential clients (scaling units), since the users who come from advertising are the same for both products, and only after entering the service they split into two categories: subscribers and one-time users.

In order to calculate the unit economics in this example, the same value should be used for the number of scaling units in the contribution margin formula. The gross profit must be calculated for each type of client separately, with its own product metrics, since all this is needed for further decision-making.

Acknowledgments

First of all, I want to express my gratitude to everyone without whom this book would not have been possible. To Ilya Krasinsky, who helped me realize that everything that I have been doing since 2008 is Data Driven. Also, thanks to him, I became acquainted with the example of "Two Palms" and, in fact, came to the term of unit economics.

I would especially like to thank Gleb Tertychny, he introduced me to Goldratt's theory of constraints that formed the basis of ueCalc's operation and helped me figure out how to create financial models for business using unit economics.

I am grateful to Dasha Shabunina, Natasha Fedotova and Alexander Eremeev for entrusting me to work with a huge number of startups in IIDF. Thanks to them, I was able to travel all over Russia and introduce unit economics to tens of thousands of people.

My gratitude to Nick Mikhailovsky — for giving me the opportunity to create a real international business that used big data for decision making. Thanks to this experience, I understood what a startup is, learned a skill of decision-making in conditions of uncertainty and understood an incredible importance of the ability to find a common language with different people.

I am particularly grateful to Masha Drobinskaya, as her multiple advice and personal assistance in difficult moments of my life were invaluable. Without her support, this book would not have been published, as she saw all my previous attempts to write this book.

Terminology

Basic model

User/Unit

The user is the basic entity that determines what we work with; in general, it is a person who became acquainted with the product through advertising. For example, this is a website visitor in case of Internet projects or a company we called during cold sales; in fact, we are talking about a card in CRM.

User/unit acquisition (UA)

Flow of acquired potential clients. It is one of the key metrics of unit economics, since it determines the flow (or number) of scaling units.

It is defined differently in different business models. For example, in classic e-commerce b2c, it is the number of unique visitors that a company attracts to its website through advertising. For complex corporate b2b business with direct sales, this is the number of new unique company records in CRM.

Conversion to first purchase (C_1)

Conversion to the first purchase. It shows what percentage of attracted scaling units become clients. It is one of the key product metrics, as it shows how well the product sells value.

It has a non-linear impact on profit margin and is often a point of business growth. It connects the space of scaling units and the space of clients:

$$LTC = CLTC \times C_1,$$
$$LTV = CLTV \times C_1$$

This metric is related to the definition of contribution margin (CM) by the formula

$$CM = UA \times (CLTV \times C_1 - LTC)$$

Buyer/Customer (B)

A client, the number of clients that the company receives from the user flow, taking the existing conversion rate into account.

$$B = UA \times C_1$$

Average Order Value (AOV)

Average check is the amount the client paid for goods or services. It can be calculated using different formulas, depending on the type of business. The one for e-commerce:

AOV = AIV × IAQ, and for the subscription model:

AOV = SUM(AIV × Share)

Average Item Value (AIV)

Average cost of one item in a cart.

Average Item Quantity (AIQ)

Average number of items in cart.

Cost of Goods Sold (COGS)

Variable costs incurred by a business at the time of a transaction. There is no clear definition of this metric, but there is a general rule that can be used to determine whether certain expenses are COGS or not: if you have zero expenses or no transactions, then it is COGS, and vice versa — if the expenses are not equal to zero (such as rent or wages), then it is not COGS.

There are two types of COGS expenses: fixed costs and costs that depend on the size of the average check. For example, the delivery cost can be fixed and the acquiring fee can be a percentage of the average bill.

First sale COGS (1sCOGS)

Additional variable costs incurred by the business at the time of the very first transaction. This type of expense typically occurs when a business incurs some expenses at the time it receives a client. However, they are not considered marketing expenses. For example, you pay a sales manager a bonus as a percentage of the first payment the client makes. Or you spend money on a compliment for a new restaurant client, expecting that the check will cover your costs.

There are two types of 1sCOGS costs: fixed costs and costs that depend on the size of the average check. For example, the delivery cost can be fixed and the acquiring fee can be a percentage of the average order value.

Average Payment Count (APC)

Average payment count per client. One of the metrics reflecting customer loyalty. It is calculated using the formula:

APC = T / B,

where T is the total number of transactions, B is the number of clients who made this number of transactions.

It is important to remember that this metric can have a significant impact on the calculation of contribution margin and to be careful when rounding this metric: rounding to two decimal places is recommended.

Minimum APC metric value = 1

Customer Lifetime Value (CLTV)

Gross profit per customer. This metric is calculated using the formula

CLTV = (AOV − COGS) × APC − 1sCOGS

Gross profit is one of the key metrics of unit economics. For example, David Skok, the author of modern unit economics, generally reduces the entire economy to only two metrics — CLTV and CAC. Essentially, this metric shows how much a business earns from a client who makes an average of APC transactions.

Despite its apparent simplicity, this metric is associated with a certain complexity. This difficulty lies in determining the time interval. Since the metric shows the value of the gross profit received from the client for APC transactions, we do not know the period at which these transactions took place. This means we have several intervals. There is a maximum period for which we can have data — this is Lifetime, the lifetime of the client, and there is the current period for which we decided to calculate the metric. If we have 12 months of data and on average one client made 10 transactions, then if we look at the CLTV for the first 5 months, our client may only make, for example, 3 transactions and, therefore, the CLTV value will be less than the one taken for the whole period of time.

Lifetime Value (LTV)

Gross profit per a scaling unit. This metric is calculated using the formula

$$LTV = CLTV \times C_1$$

The metric only appeared because marketing decisions related to scaling actually lead to an increase in the number of scaling units that are just potential customers. The percentage of potential customers that become actual customers depends on the product itself. As a result, two completely different processes are responsible for the number of clients. The first is responsible for attracting potential customers, the second - for converting them into real ones. To make decisions, you need to learn to calculate unit economics per a scaling unit. Then, the separation of CLTV and LTV becomes justified.

Customer Acquisition Cost (CAC)

Cost of marketing expenses per client. An important metric that shows the average cost of attracting one client. The importance of this metric is due to the fact that, knowing the current values of CLTV and APC as a whole for the client base, it is possible to calculate the cost of attracting a client in order to reach a given level of contribution margin (CM).

For example, on average a client brings us LTV = 10,000 rubles per APC = 10 transactions. Knowing this, you can spend, for example, 3,000 rubles to attract such a client. In this case, on the first transactions, the gross profit created by the client will be negative.

Cost per Acquisition (CPA)

Marketing costs per a scaling unit. This is the second key metric of unit economics. It allows you to determine whether a business makes money from an attracted unit or not.

The importance of this metric lies in the fact that knowing the current LTV value for the entire customer base you can calculate the cost of obtaining a scaling unit in order to reach a given level of contribution margin (CM).

For example, if the average scaling unit brings LTV = 1000 rubles, then acquisition costs of less than 1000 rubles will give a positive contribution margin. This way, you can determine which advertising channels and products are more effective and it does make sense to work with them.

Acquisition Cost (AC)

Marketing budget for attraction. This metric is calculated using the formula

$$AC = UA \times CPA = B \times CAC$$

It is a derivative metric in unit economics. It is not directly used in calculations, but in reality, the business knows how much money was spent over a period of time to attract a certain number of scaling units. At the same time, calculating the cost of attracting one unit is not easy. It's easier to take the budget and divide it by the number of units involved.

Mixed model

User acquisition for lead (UA_{LEAD})

The flow of scaling units for generation of leads in a mixed unit economics model.

The mixed model of unit economics involves calculating the contribution margin received from customers who buy attention or contacts of the audience from the company that attracts it by developing the product.

A striking example of such a model is mass media. The mass media produces content for the reader and is interested in getting the reader to return and consume the content regularly. In this case, readers usually do not pay for access to the information, but in return they see advertising placed by the advertiser.

Thus, the product works for one audience — readers (the company makes the media more convenient, simplifies access to information and spends money on attracting readers), and the business makes money by selling the attention of its audience to advertisers.

As a result, the unit economics of the mixed model is divided into two parts: the economics of the leads - those for whom the product is created and whose attention the business sells; and the economics of clients—those who buy the audience's attention.

Conversion for lead (C_{LEAD})

Conversion of scaling units into leads in a mixed unit economics model.

For the advertising model, C_{LEAD} = 100.00%, but for the lead generation model, conversion can take a value from 0.00% to 100.00%.

The lead generation model provides a service to its audience in exchange for contact information that is sold to the clients. At the same time, not all visitors leave their contacts — that is why conversion occurs.

Leads (L)

The number of leads in a mixed unit economics model is usually determined through UA_{LEAD} и C_{LEAD}.

Sale Price (SP)

Lead selling price in a mixed unit economics model. If a company sells lead contact information, then SP is the cost of one such contact. If the company has an advertising model, then SP is the cost of displaying one advertising medium to a lead.

Number of Sale (NS)

The number of sales per lead in a mixed unit economics model. In some cases, a company may sell the same lead to multiple buyers at once, such as running two or three ads at once. The higher this metric, the more the business earns per lead.

The minimum value of the NS metric = 1.

Average Requests Count for Leads (ARC$_{LEAD}$)

The average number of calls to the service per lead. It is one of the metrics showing lead loyalty.

It is important to remember that this metric can have a significant impact on the calculation of contribution margin, and to be careful when rounding it: rounding to two decimal places is recommended.

The minimum value of the ARC$_{LEAD}$ metric = 1

Cost Per Acquisition for lead (CPA$_{LEAD}$)

Cost of attracting a scaling unit in a mixed model. In a mixed model, a company sells the attention of the audience that is often attracted through advertising. CPAL shows how much a lead costs.

This metric is related to the definition of COGS$_{LEAD}$ by the formula.

$$COGS_{LEAD} = CPA_{LEAD} \times UA_{LEAD} / B$$

Acquisition Cost for lead (AC$_{LEAD}$)

Marketing budget for lead generation. This metric is calculated using the formula

$$AC_{LEAD} = UA_{LEAD} \times CPA_{LEAD}$$

This is a derivative metrics in unit economics. It is not directly used in calculations, but in reality, the business knows how much money was spent over a period of time to attract a certain number of scaling units (leads). Calculating the cost of attracting one unit is not easy; It's easier to take the budget and divide it by the number of units involved.

Inventory Release (IR)

A coefficient showing the share of leads sold. In a mixed model, a business works to increase the number of leads who use its product. However, it is not always possible to sell the entire audience. IR shows what percentage of leads a business was able to sell.

Cost of Good Sold for lead ($COGS_{LEAD}$)

Variable expenses on generating leads. In a mixed model, a business incurs costs to obtain the audience that it sells to the client. At the same time, he incurs some variable costs when making transactions with the paying party. Some of these costs relate to the cost of purchasing the leads that the business sells. If we consider the audience as a product, then $COGS_{LEAD}$ is the cost of the product.

This metric is calculated using the formula

$$COGS_{LEAD} = CPA_{LEAD} \times UA_{LEAD} / B$$

Subscription model

Lifetime (LT)

Lifetime. A universal characteristic showing how long the client lives with the product. It is measured in time units and is equal to the interval between the first and last recorded purchase at the moment.

This metric is used in revenue forecasting as well as in evaluating current advertising channels. For example, you can compare the CLTV of customers in category A for fixed periods (already generating 80% of the revenue) with current customers for the same period.

If current clients for the same LT period show worse performance than the best clients for the same time interval, then you can change the advertising campaign.

This metric is related to APC, but still those metrics are different. LT is a time interval, and APC is the number of transactions made by the client. Moreover, both metrics reflect customer loyalty.

Churn Rate (CR)

Churn rate. This is a metric showing how many customers a company retains from period to period. Typically, this metric is used to predict a customer lifetime, but it is more applicable to subscription models in which customers pay monthly (or with any other frequency). In this case, knowing the monthly outflow, you can obtain the expected number of paid periods that in the subscription model coincide with the number of APC payments using the formula:

$$APC = 1 / CR$$

However, it is not recommended to use the CR metric for a business whose customers make purchases at random intervals (as is the case with e-commerce).

Monthly Recurring Revenue (MRR)

One of the important metrics that allows you to evaluate a business with a subscription monetization model. By analyzing MRR, you can plan marketing to attract new customers, as well as work to retain existing ones. This metric is important because a modern business working with a subscription model spends more to get a client than it earns from the client in the first month, and, therefore, such a business is extremely interested in understanding how many months the client will pay. MRR allows you to evaluate the client mass as a whole.

Average Price (AvP)

Average subscription price per a tariff plan, used in subscription models.

Share

The share of customers using a particular tariff plan.

Finance

Contribution Margin (CM)

$$CM = UA \times (LTV - LTC) = UA \times (CLTV \times C_1 - LTC)$$

Unit economics helps find the required number of scaling units, the contribution margin from which covers the fixed costs of the business and allows you to reach a given level of profit.

Therefore, unit economics operates with calculation of contribution margin (CM) only. In the modern approach, a potential client (UA) is considered to be the scaling unit. And the modeling task comes down to finding the optimal configuration of metrics for calculating the contribution margin on the flow of scaling units. That is, it is necessary to find such metric values at which, firstly, contribution margin will be achievable, and secondly, the required level of contribution margin will be achieved at minimal costs.

Contribution margin can also be calculated using client metrics:

$$CM = B \times (CLTV - CLTC)$$

To reach the break-even point, contribution margin must cover fixed costs.

If the contribution margin value is positive, it is said that the unit economics converges. And the positive difference between contribution margin and fixed costs can be taken as EBITDA.

Revenue

It is a basic financial indicator that shows how much money a company receives from the customers. It is not directly used in unit economics, and is more of an informative nature.

Revenue = B × AOV × APC

Do not confuse revenue with the profit: turnover is a vanilla metric that is not applicable to data-driven decision making.

Return on Marketing Investment (ROMI)

Return on marketing investment shows how well the company spent its marketing budget. Calculated using the formula ROMI = CM / AC

Gross Profit (GP)

Gross profit. It is one of the key characteristics of a business, defined as the difference between the turnover and variable costs. In unit economics, gross profit is calculated per customer or per scaling unit. This metrics is calculated by the formula

$$CLTV = (AOV - COGS) \times APC - 1sCOGS$$

For the purposes of forecasting P&L, gross profit is calculated as the difference between the total turnover for the month and the total variable costs per month:

$$GP = Revenue - Variable\ Costs,$$

where Revenue is the sum of all transactions per month, and Variable Costs is the sum of all COGS and all 1sCOGS in these transactions.

Gross Profit Margin (GPM)

This metric is calculated by the formula

$$GPM = (Revenue - Variable\ Costs) / Revenue$$

This metric shows how much a business earns from sales as a percentage of turnover, exclusive of variable costs. For example, a business sells goods for 100,000 rubles per month, while variable costs are 75,000 rubles, so

$$GPM = (100\ 000 - 75\ 000) / 100\ 000 = 25.00\%$$

Earnings Before Interest, Taxes, Depreciation and Amortization (EBITDA)

An analytical indicator equal to the amount of profit before deduction of interest expenses, taxes, depreciation and accrued depreciation.

This indicator is calculated based on the company's financial statements and serves to assess how profitable the company's activities are without taking depreciation charges into account. This indicator is used when making comparisons with industry peers. It allows one to determine the company's performance, regardless of its debts to creditors and to the state, as well as of the depreciation method.

Net Present Value (NPV)

Net present value is the sum of the discounted values of the payment stream, reduced to the current day.

Internal Rate of Return (IRR)

Internal rate of return is the interest rate that equates the present value of future cash receipts with the value of the original investments, a net present value (NPV) is equal to zero. NPV is calculated based on the payment stream discounted to the current day.

Daniil Khanin

Unit economics
Data Driven Decisions for Business and Startups

https://khanin.info/en/books/ue--en

https://uecalc.com

daniil@khanin.info